Write a Perfect CV in a Weekend
2008 Edition

Write a Perfect CV in a Weekend

Sarah Berry

Published by
Berry Publishing

WRITE A PERFECT CV IN A WEEKEND – 2008 EDITION
A BERRY PUBLISHING BOOK

Published by:
Berry Publishing
A division of Career Consultants On-line Limited
7 Kew Lodge
226 Kew Road,
Richmond
Surrey
TW9 3LQ

1 2 3 4 5 6 7 8 9 10

ISBN 978 0 9557953 0 5

Originally published in Great Britain by Ward Lock, Cassell

PRINTING HISTORY
Ward Lock, Cassell paperback edition published 1997
Ward Lock, Cassell paperback edition published 1998
Ward Lock, Cassell paperback edition published 1999 (twice)
Berry Publishing e-book edition 2000-2003
Berry Publishing e-book edition 2003-2007 (revised)
Berry Publishing revised paperback edition 2007

Designed by Vince Wakeman
Typeset by Matt Free, Freethinking Design, Peterborough
Printed and bound in Great Britain by The Book Printing Company, Peterborough

Contents

WEEKEND TIMETABLE

Relax and pour yourself a drink – perhaps even a strong one! Now sit back and enjoy the prospect of changing the way you view your job and/or career and writing a *perfect advertisement* for yourself. You are in for the weekend of your life.

Friday

Just reading

Evening Read Chapters 1-4 and 8-10. Absorb as much of the information as you can, so that you can adopt the right approach to the rest of the weekend's work.

Saturday

Preparation

Morning Chapter 2: Complete the CV analysis test and determine how much work you have to do.

Chapter 3: Establish and work out your job targets.

Afternoon Read Chapters 5-7

Evening Time for reflection and rest, so that you are ready to put it all together on Sunday.

Sunday

Action Day

Morning and Afternoon Chapter 6: Brainstorm and then write down all your capabilities.

Chapter 4: Complete the education and personality sections.

Chapter 5: Write the technical detail on your jobs.

Chapter 7: Tell a prospective employer how valuable an employee you are.

Evening Write and type your CV. Choose a covering letter that suits the style required

You are now ready to begin your job search in earnest – may all your hard work pay off. Good luck!

4 Write a Perfect CV

ONE

Introduction to the Curriculum Vitae (CV)

Many employers are not impressed with the standard of the CVs and job applications that land on their desks. Too many are badly written, not tailored towards the job in question and do not sell the applicant. Employers therefore claim that few prospective candidates even warrant an interview.

A friend of mine, who is chairman of a multinational engineering firm, confirmed that the low standard of applications is 'sadly typical of today's job hunter'. He recently advertised a promising opportunity for a senior executive, paying a substantial salary plus a company car and fringe benefits. He was looking to appoint a qualified civil engineer, someone who was articulate, educated and well presented, and who could write error-free business material. His requirements were not unreasonably high, and he would have been prepared to interview people whose experience wasn't exactly relevant as long as they demonstrated the right qualities in their application.

'However, the process of filling the position wasn't all that simple,' says the chairman. 'Most of the CVs I received were woolly, semi-literate and poorly presented. Many looked as if they had been thrown together in a rush and were full of spelling mistakes. Some ignored the request for salary details altogether and a few applicants didn't even bother to enclose a CV, sending only a letter outlining their details.' This employer's overwhelming impression was that most applications represented a desperate plea for a job. Candidates had not tailored their applications to the job on offer, or said why their experience and expertise would benefit his company.

This example is not a one-off case, and it is quite normal for employers to reject hundreds of mediocre, poor and substandard applications. Often the end result is that the employer is faced with the frustrating task of re-advertising the position at further expense.

TOP TEN REASONS

WHY EMPLOYERS REJECT CVS/JOB APPLICATIONS

As indicated above, most candidates don't even get as far as the interview stage. They are dropped from the selection process because their CV and/or application is not good enough. The top ten reasons for rejection are:

1. **The presentation is of a low standard.**
   The application includes errors, spelling mistakes, is presented using simple text editors rather than a standard word-processing package such as Word. Most employers say that they haven't the time to read each application in great detail and simply give each one a quick once-over. When asked how long this might take their answers ranged from 20 seconds to two minutes – so first impressions do count.

2. **The content does not comply with requests.**
   You need to do what is asked, not just as you wish. If you have been sent an application form, fill it in: don't be tempted simply to put 'see attached CV'. If the form asks for salary details, give them; likewise with photographs. Don't try to be clever or funny - it rarely works (so don't provide photographs in amusing locations or attire). If the applicant doesn't comply with the requests, the employer will see him/her as someone who will be difficult to control.

3. **The application is not tailored to the job in question.**
   You will need to explain in your CV why your experience is relevant and why you would be a good choice for the

particular job. Most CVs give only a list of duties and jobs done, but companies are result and profit orientated and so employers are looking for people who achieve within their roles.

4. **The CV makes outrageous claims of success.**
   Don't be tempted to make something sound more impressive than it really is. You may be brilliant and have done an excellent job, but don't exaggerate. Employers will see through this approach.

5. **The CV is full of discrepancies.**
   For example, there may a difference between the candidate's age and date of birth. Discrepancies demonstrate that the applicant has a sloppy attitude because he/she can't be bothered to update the CV.

6. **There is no covering letter.**
   A covering letter is an absolute must, but it must say more than just that the 'CV is attached'. It should be effective and should summarize your key capabilities and strengths, demonstrating to the employer how he/she would benefit by taking you on.

7. **The application is rejected because of some form of prejudice**.
   This could include reasons such as:

   - You are female or male.
   - You are too young or too old.
   - You haven't attended a particular educational establishment.
   - You have a foreign or strange-sounding name.
   - For some reason the application threatens the prospective employer.

Sadly, prejudice will always exist. Indeed, I am sure that we have all been guilty, at some time, of making snap decisions or judgements based upon some kind of prejudice. However, to be a successful job hunter you need to spend time only on those things that you can actively influence: your CV/application, your appearance and, most importantly, your attitude. These play a far greater part in whether or not you are successful than does the fact that you are in a so-called minority or disadvantaged sector. So, try to accept the existence of prejudice and continue to present yourself in best possible light. Don't give up or get angry, or upset about it - if you continue to highlight your skills and capabilities and present yourself in a positive light, you will get the job you desire in the end.

8. **The position is no longer available.**
   Sometimes the employer's requirements change and so the recruitment process is stopped. You can never influence this situation.

9. **The applicant does not have relevant qualifications or experience.**
   You may already know this, but it could be that you haven't yet learned how to present yourself properly.

10. **The applicant does not have the right attitude.**
    Attitude is reflected in the tone of your CV as well as in the interview. The ultimate job decision is based upon the employer's gut feeling about your attitude and this is where many candidates trip up, as they fail to realize the importance of this aspect. We are not talking about being a bit tired of filling out piles of forms or attending interviews, answering the same types of questions over and over again, but something much deeper. You may actually feel reasonably happy inside - but are you aware that the vocabulary you choose when you write your application, your facial expression when you convey your message in your interview,

your behaviour, your dress sense and more all goes to make up 'attitude'. In fact, attitude speaks even more loudly than what you say. The true test of your attitude is to see it in action. Take a look in the mirror, or video a dummy interview. Is this the real you? Do you like what you see? Is your attitude making others warm to you or withdraw from you? All this will be reflected in the way you prepare your CV and job application.

For example:

☒ **A sloppy attitude** could be assumed if the CV is poorly presented and full of mistakes, and a covering letter is not included.

☒ **A desperate attitude** might be reflected in a covering letter which focuses on the individual's difficult state of affairs (divorce, bereavement etc) rather than on the employer.

☒ **An angry attitude** could be detected if the covering letter or CV places blame with others for things that have gone wrong or that the candidate should have done.

☒ **An irrational attitude** could be suspected if the candidate does not have the qualifications that the advertisement is asking for, or if things aren't explained in the covering letter - perhaps the candidate lives in Scotland but is applying for a job in South Wales and the employer will want to know the reason why, otherwise he/she might make one up (and it may not be the right one!)

☒ **A know-it-all attitude** will be suspected if the covering letter tells the company that the candidate can sort out all its problems before he/she even knows whether or not it has any!

Employers want to employ people, fill their positions and offer people careers. They do not necessarily want to employ the most highly qualified person, but they do want to hire the right person for the job and are therefore interested in the whole person - the candidate's personality and interests - but from most of the applications they receive the candidate appears 'faceless' and thus not worth interviewing. Most applications do nothing more than give a list of the applicant's previous job titles and duties - they don't tell the employer what the person has achieved within their role, what they added to the company, or how they improved their job/situation.

It is hardly surprising, therefore, that most applications receive very little attention from the employer before they are tossed into the 'No' pile. The message from employers is that most job hunters just can't get it right, so those that do, stand a far greater chance of success.

Your CV

Most advertisements ask you to reply by sending in a full, current and comprehensive CV. However, having to prepare, write and type up a good CV is a grim task for most job hunters. It is something they would rather not have to do, especially in their precious spare time, so the way they get around it is to do a poor job. If it is a first-time CV, candidates often copy the format, style and disasters of a friend's CV. Otherwise, most candidates drag out their old CV, give it a quick read through to see if it will do, update if necessary and then send it in. They may even go as far as getting it typed up into a new format and perhaps giving it a bit of 'oomph' by adding a three-line character resumé of themselves along the lines of 'I am a brilliant communicator, work hard under pressure and can manage people'.

Yes, it's true; most CVs are written in this way and this is why employers are so disappointed by them. In fact, an employer once told me that he felt he would get a better response from candidates if the advertisement asked for 'your most boring CV ever; send it in full of as much drivel and information on yourself as possible; hand-written or typed in whatever format takes your fancy; with or without mistakes; with lots of lists and minor details about tasks done, and include as many clichés as you think are relevant - good communicator, goal orientated, honest and ambitious - but please don't back them up because it is fun for us to do that for you!' 'Would you get a better response?' I asked, amazed by his tongue in-cheek approach. 'Yes', he replied, 'Because most of the faint-hearted job hunters would be put off applying, and those who did would make a bigger effort than usual to write a decent CV. Then at least I would be spared the task of reading hundreds of boring ones.' So, if you are tempted to think that writing a CV is a bore, spare a thought for the poor person having to read it.

REASONS FOR A POOR CV

Most people are not particularly good at CV writing, although research shows that most believe that they are. It is not so much that they don't know what to write, because most people have a rough idea of what to include, but that they are out of touch with presenting themselves in modern and competitive terms and thus winning over the employer.

Modern CVs have evolved over time. There are no written laws or guidelines on CV writing, it is something which is very personal and of course subject to fashion. Thirty or forty years ago all that was required of you was to write a brief letter, including relevant details about yourself and why you thought you could do the job on offer. Now the trend is to put *everything* down on paper - from graphic personal details including operations you may have had, to every course that you have ever attended - even if it is irrelevant.

Evidence that today's job hunter cannot write an effective CV can be found in the fact that many employers still cling to their standard application form because it overcomes the CV hurdle. The reasons behind a poor CV include:

1. **Lack of knowledge.**

   The fundamental problem is that candidates are unaware of what makes up a good and effective CV. Lack of knowledge is 90 per cent of the problem and the remaining 10 per cent is lack of understanding of how to use that knowledge in the right way. Most job hunters have only limited experience of looking for work, as this is something that happens only a few times in their career. In the beginning, simply having a job is what matters and you may get away with a poorer CV/ application, but, as you advance along the career path, securing the best possible job becomes more important and your application has to be of a high standard.

2. **Lack of time.**

   The biggest handicap for job hunters is the lack of time. Most do not have the time to study the subject of job hunting in detail before they embark on their approach - and they probably don't have the inclination either! They want to secure a job quickly, perhaps to escape from their current job situation or to advance their career again after a static period. Consequently, as time and experience are lacking their approach is often somewhat haphazard, and they take neither the time nor the energy to reflect upon their success rate.

   However, if you know what works as far as CVs/applications and covering letters are concerned you will save time in the long run, because you will have fewer to write. You don't want to do what you have always done willy-nilly, and you will know from experience that this is not the most efficient approach.

3. **The applicant has never seen a good CV.**

   Unless you are or have been in the position of hiring people, you will probably never have seen a good CV and realized how it stands out. You therefore have nothing on which to base the writing of your own CV.

4. **The CV is not tailored to the job in question.**

   Most CVs commit the same sin: they are full of historical detail, some relevant and some irrelevant, and they do not answer the prospective employer's fundamental question of whether or not you are capable of doing the job and what value you would offer to the company. In fact, most of the CVs employers receive have little or no connection to the company at all.

5. **The CV does not sell the applicant.**

   Most CVs do nothing more than list personal details and job duties. What they don't do is advertise the applicant's key capabilities and strengths and convince the prospective employer that this person deserves an interview. This is a tricky balance, but this book will show you how to achieve it.

Your CV is the crucial aspect of your job hunt. It is your admission ticket into the job market: it is your chance to sing your own praises, to demonstrate your personal and work-related achievements, and to get a foot in the door. While a good CV won't necessarily get you the job, a poor CV will see you dropped from the selection process time and time again.

A GOOD CV SHOULD

1. Be easy to read and follow.
2. Be letter perfect.
3. Sell you, your capabilities and achievements.
4. Be three pages or less in length.
5. Be well organized and easy to understand.
6. Give the reader an idea of your personality.
7. Demonstrate the benefit of taking you on.
8. Be well presented and neat.
9. Be informative but not chatty.
10. Get you an interview!

In Chapter 2 you will have a chance to put your current CV to the test, to see how good it is and whether it is doing its job properly. Your CV will be given a score out of 100, and you will then have an indication of how employers perceive it and will know which areas you need to improve in order to increase its effectiveness.

THIS BOOK WILL DEMONSTRATE

1. **How to take control of your job hunt.**
   By preparing an individual, targeted CV you will be able to see yourself in your chosen field.
2. **The weaknesses of your current CV.**
   You will see what is putting off employers from inviting you to attend an interview. You will then know which sections of the CV you need to spend time improving.
3. **How to present yourself in the best possible light.**
   This is essential if, for example, you don't have the exact qualifications the advertisement is asking for, have been out of work for a long time or have worked for the same company all your working life.
4. **Thc most successful CV format.**
   You want to avoid putting off the employer because your CV style or format is not appealing.
5. **How to sell yourself and make yourself look a winner.**
   Never assume that your value is known. Employers are looking for certain qualities, which you will need to convey.
6. **How to target your application towards each employer.**
   An all-round, general-purpose CV is out of the question. This book will show you how to target your CV to the job on offer. The benefit to you will be that you will be in charge of your work-search campaign and your CV will therefore be dramatically more successful.
7. **How to write about your work experience and education in an interesting way.** Most CVs are dull and send prospective employers to sleep.
8. **That you can write a winning CV in a short period of time as long as you are aware of what to include.**

TWO

The CV Analysis Test

This chapter answers two fundamental questions:

How good is your CV?

Is your CV doing its job properly?

When I ask my clients these questions at the introductory career session, they typically answer that, on the whole, they think their CV is OK, but it may need a bit of improvement here and there. Most then admit that they have used the same format, style and tone of CV for years, but while it may have won them an interview a few years ago it is no longer being as effective in the current job market.

The crucial test, though, is what the employer thinks about your CV. If you are not selected for an interview on the basis of your CV, it is tempting to make up your own explanations. You may put it down to your age, marital status, education, work experience, job title, salary, race, sex or current company, but are these the real reasons? Probably not. It is true that these factors may play a part, but the answer is usually much deeper than this.

Anyone, whatever their ability, can project themselves in a positive, honest way that will win them work. The secret is knowing how to sell yourself and convince the employer that you should be invited to attend an interview. So your CV needs to:

☑ **Be targeted to the job.** Tailor the CV to the position on offer. Throw out the general CV.

☑ **Show you are capable of doing the job.** Demonstrate briefly and quickly your key skills and capabilities. The employer doesn't want to plough through reams of paper in order to answer the question 'Can this person do the job?'

☑ **List your accomplishments.** Highlight what you have achieved within your job and convince the employer that you would be a good choice.

☑ **Show that you have 'personality'.** Convey what sort of person you are.

☑ **Reflect your attitude.** Keep the tone on a straightforward, positive and businesslike level. Don't dwell on why you left a job, as this will only create doubt in the employer's mind about your abilities.

☑ **Be brief and to the point.** Only include relevant information - your spouse's name does not reflect your ability to do the job, so keep personal details down to a minimum. Never express in ten words what can be said in four.

☑ **Demonstrate that you believe in yourself.** Advertise yourself - the whole person - rather than giving lots of lists of information.

☑ **Be written and presented in a professional way.** You cannot afford to send out a CV which contains grammatical errors or spelling mistakes, or which is simply scruffy.

A good CV is one that is effective, solid and balanced in all areas. Most are not, but it is not until this is pointed out that the candidate becomes aware of the deficiencies in his/her own CV.

Taking the test

You now have the opportunity to assess your existing CV. This will enable you to see how employers, who have never met you before, perceive you when they read your CV for the first time. Is it portraying the best possible image of you? Put your CV through the test and find out if it is strong in all areas. If it fails to show you off in the best possible light then you need a new CV, fast - one which 'sells' you to your highest potential.

To complete the test, read through each question and think about the answer. You will need to refer to your CV, so have it to hand. When you have decided whether the answer is yes or no, put the corresponding score in the score box on the right-hand side. You may find it easier if you cross out the irrelevant answer to avoid confusion.

If you answer 'yes' to any of the questions below, it would be a good idea to get a friend or someone you trust to complete the test on your behalf.

☑ Do you tend to be too generous with scoring?

☑ Do you find it difficult to detach yourself from the emotional side?

☑ Do you want a ***truly*** honest and independent viewpoint?

☑ Do you find decision-making difficult?

☑ Do you find it difficult to see things unless they are pointed out?

When you have answered every question, add up the scores under each of the five headings and put each total on the score sheet. Add up all these scores to give a total mark out of 100.

Most of my clients score between 25 and 40 out of 100. In fact, I have only ever had a handful of clients score over 50, and even then their CV needed improvement in certain areas to enable them to reach their full potential. The score guidelines are there to indicate the areas in which your CV is either strong or weak. In my experience, most people have average marks in the presentation and layout, accuracy and content sections, but score either nothing or very little in the effectiveness and style and personality sections.

If you would like to receive an unbiased professional assessment of your CV and covering letter visit www.perfectcv.com

CV analysis test

A good CV is worth whatever time and effort it takes.

A Presentation and Layout

Is the title Curriculum Vitae or CV included as a header?
The CV is about you, so all that is necessary is your name.

Yes 0 No 1
SCORE

Is the CV too long?
Ideally, a CV should be three pages or less. Remember that to say less is in fact to say more.

Yes 0 No 5
SCORE

Does it have consistent spacing?
Check and count the number of lines between paragraphs and sections. The margins to the top, bottom, left- and right-hand side of the page should be the same, ideally 2.5cm (1 in).

Yes 3 No 0
SCORE

Is it easy to use as an interview document?
Is the information under the right section and is it all in one place? Some CVs have two personal details sections, one at the beginning and another at the end. This immediately begs the question: what is this person trying to hide? It is much easier to understand a CV if sections are not split between pages. The personal details and education sections should certainly not be split between pages, and you should only split up the work experience if absolutely necessary. In this case, start each job on a new page, and don't carry a bit of one job over on to another page. The interviewer doesn't want to be flicking over the pages all the time or be faced with having seen something but then be unable to find it again. Logical ordering of information is absolutely essential.

Yes 5 No 0
SCORE

Is it easy to follow?
This refers especially to dates of education and employment. Don't be tempted to think you can get away with covering up the fact that you retook some examinations, had a career break or took a year to find another job. Hiding things rarely works. Relax: career gaps, moves and changes in direction can all be explained in a positive and honest way.

Yes 5 No 0
SCORE

Does the CV include a binder, photograph or fussy material?
Include these items only if they have been asked for. A good CV will stand out on its own - it is not necessary to resort to tacky techniques. Anyway, you can show the interviewer how good-looking you are when you get there!

Yes 0 No 1
SCORE

Does it include long and rambling sentences?
A sentence longer than 12 words is pushing the reader's concentration a bit, so keep sentence length down.

Yes 0 No 2
SCORE

Was the CV produced using a standard software package such as Word?
Employer's use standard software packages such as Word. Make sure you follow the standards. There is nothing worse than the recipient not being able to open your file!

Yes 1 No 0
SCORE

Was it easy to print?
Make sure the content doesn't disappear off into the margins when you print the file.

Yes 1 No 0
SCORE

Is it well typed?
Ensure that your CV is typed, and typed well. If you don't type you should not attempt it, because a poor result is not worth the effort. Have your CV typed up professionally instead.

Yes 1 No 0
SCORE

Is the typeface suitable?
A suitable typeface is Times Roman or a similar business font. The size should be 10 or 11 point, depending on the printer. As a check for size, with 2.5cm (1 in) left- and right-hand margins there should be 15-18 words on a line.

Yes 1 No 0
SCORE

B Accuracy

Does the CV have any spelling mistakes?
Most CVs do, but if they had been properly checked they wouldn't!

Yes 0 No 3
SCORE

Is it written in the third person singular?
The third person singular is the usual and more powerful style for CV writing.

Yes 2 No 0
SCORE

Does it include any clichés, jargon or slang?
Your aim is to include, not exclude, the reader, so cut out the jargon and clarify where necessary.

Yes 0 No 1
SCORE

Are all the sentences constructed correctly?
Do your sentences include verbs? It is amazing how many people leave out verbs, adjectives and nouns when writing a CV.

Yes 1 No 0
SCORE

Are they punctuated correctly?
It is a chore, but do check.

Yes 1 No 0
SCORE

Do they include active words?
Words like solved, performed, redirected, developed, implemented, sold, supervised, increased and so on create a positive impression. You will have an opportunity to choose and use key words such as these on page 89.

Yes 6 No 0
SCORE

Does the CV clarify abbreviations?
It is important to do this, otherwise you could be rejected on a misinterpretation of information.

Yes 1 No 0
SCORE

Does it repeat words, facts, or thoughts?
Once is quite enough for the reader!

Yes 0 No 1
SCORE

C Content

Is your preferred name used?
Use your preferred name, otherwise you will be putting yourself at an immediate disadvantage. For example, use Dave instead of David or Debbie instead of Deborah.

Yes 1 No 0
SCORE

Does the CV include full postal address, telephone number and email address?
If you want to receive a telephone call or email in response, include these details.

Yes 1 No 0
SCORE

Does the CV include any irrelevant information, such as:

Place of birth

Yes 0 No 1
SCORE

Children's names and ages

Yes 0 No 1
SCORE

Spouse's name

Yes 0 No 1
SCORE

Referees

Yes 0 No 1
SCORE

Religion

Yes 0 No 1
SCORE

Hobbies

Yes 0 No 1
SCORE

Salary/benefits

Yes 0 No 1
SCORE

This type of information does not add anything to the CV, so be brave and leave it out!

Is sufficient educational detail included?
For example, the qualification obtained, the educational establishment, dates and the course or level studied.

Yes 2 No 0
SCORE

Is a covering letter included with the CV for this analysis test?
A covering letter is as important as the CV itself. It can be used to clarify certain aspects of your expertise or to sell other qualities.

Yes 2 No 0
SCORE

Does the CV cover all important facts?
Does it answer the questions how, what, why, when and who?

Yes 6 No 0
SCORE

D Effectiveness

Is the CV geared towards a job target or field of work?

Yes 6 No 0
SCORE

Does the CV give the reader a clear idea of what job you are looking for? You cannot get away with thinking that a job might be what you are looking for and so you apply for it: you need to have an active approach to job hunting. Think about and decide upon the type of company you want to work for and work you wish to be doing, and the income you would like to be earning. Then you can target your CV at only those companies you believe are suitable.

Does the CV emphasize your relevant skills?

Yes 5 No 0
SCORE

A job advertisement highlights the level and kind of skills that the company is seeking. Most CVs, however, do not stress and highlight the person's skills. The skills may be there, but they are usually bunched up and hidden under the duties section. The candidate is therefore relying on the reader's intelligence and interest to discover them, and most employers do not want to go through a CV with a highlighter pen picking out the relevant bits. The appropriate presentation of skills should be done by the candidate (see Chapter 6).

Is the CV selling you? Does it stress accomplishments over skills and duties?

Yes 5 No 0
SCORE

A duty is a duty. Just because you have done a job for so many months or years means nothing: what counts is results. A duty is not a result, it is your obligation to the company; it is what you get paid to do each day, month and year. What sells you is your achievements - what you did in the job that added value to the company. Achievements don't have to be amazing but they must be yours, so include anything that demonstrates your unique contribution to a company (for example, contributing ideas, advising on matters, making presentations, inventing things or acquiring new business).

Is the CV written in the employer's language?
If not, why not? Take your cue from the wording in the advertisement or application form. Does it use short, snappy sentences? Or technical terms? Or use terms that are looking for creative ideas?

Yes 1 No 0
SCORE

Does the CV show that you have thought carefully about the job before applying for it?
A personalized letter will be read before a mail-shot one, so make your CV personal by picking up on references made in the advertisement and backing this up with detailed explanations.

Yes 1 No 0
SCORE

Does the CV demonstrate how the employer will benefit from taking you on?
This is difficult to do well. Most covering letters get around this hurdle by stating that the person can help sort out all the company's problems (see page 12) or that this company needs this person. Why? Employers are not impressed with this pushy and brash approach, and it rarely works. Demonstrate your worth by highlighting your skills, achievements and work experience. An employer will then be interested in you because he/she will see that you can add value to his/her company.

Yes 1 No 0
SCORE

Is the CV exciting to read?
If someone has to re-read something or cannot retain the information without having to refer back to the document then the CV cannot be classified as an exciting read! It is possible to make a historical, factual and personal document interesting to read if you:

Yes 1 No 0
SCORE

☑ Choose active rather than passive verbs.

☑ Keep the CV to two pages or less.

☑ Stress skills and accomplishments.

☑ Type and present it in a professional way.

☑ Personalize each CV for the job in question.

E Style and Personality

Does the CV reflect your personality?
Much of an employer's final decision is based upon personality. For example, will you fit in with the team, and will customers and clients warm to you? Personality can be portrayed in the capabilities section of your CV by expressing your five most saleable qualities - qualities that are crucial to you as a person including your personality in your CV will greatly enhance your chances of success.

Yes 6 No 0
SCORE

Does the CV emphasize your job capabilities?
You cannot get away with simply giving a list of duties performed. If the CV includes *all* your relevant capabilities you stand a greater chance of success. For example, the job advertisement may not mention presentation skills and you may only ever have to present a handful of times, but if you include this as one of your capabilities you will immediately draw a distinction between yourself and the hundreds of other candidates who leave it out because it hasn't been asked for. So, don't be shy when you fill in your capabilities in Chapter 6, because thoroughness is what is required. In this way, the employer's omission could work to your advantage.

Yes 6 No 0
SCORE

Does the CV show that you have researched the company and job?
An exact match of experience and company background are not required, but it will need to be similar. It is harder to move from a smaller company to a multinational one than the other way round, so check out the company beforehand and target your application accordingly.

Yes 1 No 0
SCORE

Does the CV reflect a positive image of you?
A positive attitude will help you succeed. If you feel good in yourself, you will influence your environment positively and employers will want to hire you: no employer wants to hire a tired, negative person with a gloomy outlook on life. A positive image on paper will inspire the employer to have faith in your worth and the valuable contribution you can make to a company. To achieve this you will need to use active words rather than weak ones, especially in the capabilities section of the CV (see page 89). Be honest in your descriptions, and if you find it difficult enlist the support of a friend or family member. If your CV doesn't meet the positive criteria it will fail to show you off in your best light and you will miss out.

Yes 5 No 0
SCORE

Yes 1 No 0
SCORE

Does the CV show that you enjoy work and life?
Most CVs do either one thing or the other, not both. It is difficult to balance the two in a CV, but it is essential to do so. No one wants to admit that they are a work bore and have done nothing other than work, work and more work, yet many CVs overplay the importance of working long hours and weekends. On the other hand it is dangerous if you state or imply that your job doesn't really matter that much to you, perhaps by including a long list of demanding hobbies. Your job would matter to you if you were suddenly made redundant, so play it safe and leave the hobbies question for the interview. Then, if you see a picture of the interviewer on his/her desk taking part in your preferred sport, you can start up a conversation on an area of mutual interest. However, try to include at least one personal capability demonstrating that you have something about you other than work. For example, you may want to mention your sense of humour, positive outlook or enjoyment of travel.

SCORING

	Maximum Score	Your Score
Presentation and Layout	26	________
Accuracy	16	________
Content	19	________
Effectiveness	20	________
Style and Personality	19	________
Total	100	

RATINGS

Score 0-30 **Weak**

Your CV is putting you at a disadvantage in relation to other candidates. It lacks essential detail and is 'sloppy' regarding accuracy. The chances of being asked for an interview are slim. You may find that the questions you are asked at an interview are more difficult or negative than those asked of candidates with better CVs.

Score 31-50 **Average**

Your CV is of average quality but lacks direction. It conforms to most employers' basic requirements but gives you no advantage over other candidates. It is also narrowing your career opportunities. By improving your CV, you may be able to advance your career more quickly or widen your experience.

Score 51-80 **Good**

Your CV is giving you an advantage over other candidates with the same experience and skills as yourself. However, you may not be realizing your full potential. It is likely that your CV is narrowing your options to fields of work that you have previously worked in, or is enabling you to take only small steps in advancing your career or changing direction. You need to strengthen your CV so that it reflects your personality and demonstrates your job capabilities.

Score 81-100 **Excellent**

Your CV is enabling you to apply for jobs with confidence. You are demonstrating to an employer how you can benefit his company, as well as indicating your career plans. By continuing to focus on the opportunities open to you, raising your profile and developing your interview skills, you will be able to give yourself new career opportunities.

The worst part of losing a job over a weak CV is that it is the one aspect of your job search over which you have complete control. If it fails to show you off in the best light, you are doing yourself a grave disservice.

A typical CV is shown on the next page. The errors are marked with superscript numbers and explained in the notes that follow, and it has been put through the analysis test to show you exactly how this works.

A TYPICAL CV FULL OF ERRORS

Curriculum Vitae[1]

Name:[2] John Smith
Home address: [3,4] 12 Longlevens Avenue
Canterbury Kent
Telephone: Home 01227 1253
Work[5] 01227 6821
Date of birth:[6] 30 April 1967
Age:[6] 40
Marital Status: Married, 2 children (Peter and Elizabeth) [7]
Height & Weight: 6ft 2in, 12 stone 6 oz[8]

Personal Profile: An outstanding leader who is dynamic, hard-working, proactive, empathetic and committed, with excellent communication skills at all levels and a proven track record of delivering results. [9]

Qualifications: [10]

'O' Levels: Ten (including English and Maths)

'A' Levels: 3 (Economics (B) Geography (B), General Studies (D)

Degree: BA (Hons) Business Studies (Finance) Upper Second classification

Accountancy qualification: ACMA

All first-time passes finished 1991, accepted as member 1994

Current employer: [11]

Ogden Assurance Ltd, London

6 Park Street

London[11]

June[12] 1997 to present

Current salary: £44,495 plus office allowance, 6% bonus, car and subsidised mortgage.[13]

Work History

Current Position:

Finance Manager, Ogden, London[14]

Responsibities:[15]

February 2000 to present

Home Service Systems provides a mainframe and network service throughout Odgen, its primary customer is Home Service. It currently employs 700 staff and has annual expenditure of approximately £85 million. My role covers the following: responsible for the production of the monthly management accounts, Key performance indicators (KPIs), invoicing of internal customers and collection of cash, accounts payables, quarterly returns, and Year-end consolidation schedules, VAT returns and Benefit in Kind reporting.

Responsible for the co-ordination and production of the HSS budget process

Managing the Managing the HSS Sales ledger including the production of Internal billing invoices, the collection of cash from our customers and provision of detailed resource usage statistics (PMFs).

Responsible for Accounts payable function, including payment of suppliers and reimbursement of expenses via BACS.

Additionally I[16] have been responsible for the implementation of a new accounting system using a package called Chameleon which runs on a UNIX operating system.

More recently I[16] have been responsible for transferring HSS accounting to a mainframe package, MARS a bespoke derivative of Dun and Bradstreet's general ledger GL:M and Accounts Payable AP:M packages.

Responsible for the nomina ledger, including Balance Sheet and cashbook including the receipt of cash, (HSS has a separate bank account), manual cheques for items over £50,000, foreign currency and the associated accounting.

Report to the Business Processing Financial Controller.

Manage a total staff of 12 which comprises 2 qualified accountants, 1 part-qualified accountant 1 finance graduate 1 IS grade and 7 clerical staff.

Previous positions within Ogden:[17]

Ogden Life and Pensions

Finance Manager

7 staff

July[12] 1999 to January[12] 2000

Odgen Portfolio Managers

Financial Accountant

2 staff

November[12] 1998 to June[12] 1999

Odgen Portfolio Managers

Project Accountant

June[12] 1997 to October[12] 1998

Previous employment:

Monterrey Ltd, London

32 staff, salary on leaving: £28,600+bonus+car[13]

Commercial Manager, October[12] 1995 to May[12] 1997

ICQ Ltd, London

Branch Finance and Commercial Controller, 16 staff + involvement in merging of two branches

Salary on leaving: £24,750[14], October[12] 1994 to October[12] 1995

Regional Revenue Controller, May 1993[12] to October 1994[12]

Kuba Ltd, London

International Internal Auditor, August[12] 1992 to April[12] 1993, salary on leaving: £19,500[13]

Lolima Ltd, London

Finance graduate trainee, September[12] 1989 to July[12] 1992, salary on leaving £17,200[13]

Personal Details: Health excellent, clean driving licence[19]

Interests: Roller coasters, wreck diving, fine wine.[19]

1. **'Curriculum Vitae'** – Prospective employers will be able to recognise from its overall design and structure that this is a CV, John, so it isn't necessary to label the document formally as being one. Therefore, the first item that should appear at the top of the page would be your name.
2. **'Name:'** Most data labels (such as the word 'Name') are not needed in a CV, John, since prospective employers will be used to seeing large numbers of CVs and will be able to guess correctly from the context and placement what each of the details provided represents. When they see 'John Smith' at the top of the first page, they'll immediately recognise it as being your name.
3. **'Home address:'** Here also, John, it's not necessary to use a data label … you can just state your address. But you should add your postcode to it so that there will be no delay in reaching you (for those employers who still prefer to use snail mail when contacting applicants).
4. Nowadays prospective employers are increasingly using email to contact job applicants, John, so I would also include your email address here (in addition to your other contact details) so you won't miss out on possible job opportunities.
5. The type style for the word '**Work**' is not the same as for word 'Home', John, and the two are misaligned.
6. It isn't necessary to include both your date of birth and your age in your CV, John. The Age Discrimination Legislation introduced on 1st October 2006 means that putting either of the two down is now optional. But if you do choose to list one of them here, it's better to mention your age rather than your date of birth as that way prospective employers won't be tempted to waste a portion of your review time allotment by stopping to calculate your age mentally.
7. Your children's names aren't needed in your CV, John.
8. Your height and weight aren't needed in your CV either.
9. Profile sections are common in CVs, John, but they're much too limited to have any real selling power (they're the CV equivalent of the very short political adverts during elections

which talk the candidate up and are very complimentary but which provide few useful details). As a result, employers are unlikely to be wowed, especially if your CV is the 135th one in their stack that day with this same approach and using similar phrasing. What employers will be looking to learn here will be much more specific: what can you do for them, how would you do it, what is notable about your approach and how you would use each specific skill to benefit your next employer? For example, a large majority of CVs will claim to have excellent communication skills, so making that same claim in yours won't be taken at face value unless you back it up with specifics. What is your communication style? How would you tailor it to specific types of work situations? How would you use it to gain a business advantage for your next employer? How would you use it to influence others? How is your communication style more effective than what your peers might do? And so on … details such as those will be of more interest to employers. Put differently, prospective employers will look to hire the applicant who will make them more money … how are you going to do this? And as a side comment, you also include one of the most overused CV clichés here, which is that you have a "proven track record", and that one won't sway an employer. Whilst it's true that many job adverts mention that they're looking for someone with proven ability or a proven track record, those employers aren't looking for assurance that you're this person (they'll see that as just 'parroting back the advert'). Rather, they're asking you to provide the proof.

10. Your qualifications section is not well-organised and it's also lacking several details, such as the name and location of the school(s) for each of the academic qualifications completed and the year in which each had been awarded. And what have you been doing since then to stay abreast of developments in the business world in general and in your area of speciality in particular? Prospective employers will also be looking here to learn about that aspect of your training and development.

11. You won't need to provide a full address for any of your past employers, John. However, I would merge this section into the next section, as prospective employers will want to look at all of your work-related content within a single, logically-organised section for their ease of review.
12. You won't need to indicate the actual months anywhere in your CV, John, as that just adds clutter to your CV. What prospective employers will be looking to get at this point in the recruiting process will be just 'the big picture', so it's quite acceptable to show each date in your CV in terms of the year rather than the month and year.
13. From a negotiating standpoint, John, you'll have a stronger hand if you create interest in yourself first and broach the topic of compensation only much later on in the recruiting process. Therefore I would leave out any mention of salary from your CV. If an employer specifically requests your salary details, then I'd provide the information, but only in the covering letter to that employer (and not in the CV itself).
14. Prospective employers will want to see a bit of context for your past employer before reviewing your responsibilities for that role, John. What does Ogden do? What do they make and sell? Where do they operate? What's unique or special about them? How big are they?
15. This section accounts for your time, John, and it shows the range of your experience, but it isn't doing anything to market you. Here's the problem: you describe the job itself but not the specific excellence of your performance in that role. In other words, just how good (specifically) were you at your job? How did you make a personal difference? What was special about your work? How did you add specific value? What did you bring to this role that your predecessor did not? What did you do on the job that was innovative? How did you get more out of any technology that you used on the job than did many of your peers at the time? And so on. At the most basic level, employers understand that (by definition) half of all workers in any job category were below average whilst the other half were above average (and they'll

want to hire from the second group when possible). What specific examples of your work would show prospective employers how and why you belong in that second group?

16. Your CV should be written in the implied third person rather than in the first person, John..
17. Prospective employers will want to see full job details for each of your earlier roles as well, John, including a summary of responsibilities for that role and specific achievements that you had delivered to that employer.

Other Observations: Prospective employers will spend not more than about twenty seconds with your CV before making their 'keep or toss' decision, John, so I'd switch to a blend of narrative and bullet-point formats in your CV to anticipate that typical employer reviewing style. In addition, your CV uses several of the more commonly overused CV buzz words and buzz phrases that become stale for employers seeing them repeated in most of the CVs that they receive and review. You also have a number of minor grammatical and typing errors, inconsistencies (especially in the use of upper and lower case letters) and spelling errors (such as the name 'Ogden' having been miswritten as 'Odgen' in three spots), and that will work against you when it comes to making that all-important strong first impression on prospective employers. They'll look to your CV not just for the factual content but also as a mini-audition for how effectively you can work, how efficiently you can think, your attention to detail, your ability to organise content and so on, and this CV will not fare well in that audition.

Overall Comment: What most stands out in your CV, John, is that it's underpowered. The two most important areas (in terms of potential selling power) are your experience and your skills, and although you have some good experience, you focus on process in your work history (but then say nothing about any specific achievements you had delivered) and you say far too little about transferable skills that you'll bring to your next role. Prospective employers reviewing your CV will be most interested in the topic of 'value' … how would you deliver specific value to them in your next role (if they do add you to their team) and how have you done the same in past roles for your past employers? To stand out, therefore, you need to translate your work experience, training and qualifications, skills and working style into benefits for your next employer and your CV doesn't do that now.

JOHN SMITH'S CV ANALYSIS TEST

A Presentation and Layout

Is the title Curriculum Vitae or CV included as a header?	Yes 0 No 1	SCORE *0*
Is the CV too long?	Yes 0 No 5	SCORE *5*
Does it have consistent spacing?	Yes 3 No 0	SCORE *0*
Is it easy to use as an interview document?	Yes 5 No 0	SCORE *0*
Is it easy to follow?	Yes 5 No 0	SCORE *0*
Does the CV include a binder, photograph or fussy material?	Yes 0 No 1	SCORE *1*
Does it include long and rambling sentences?	Yes 0 No 2	SCORE *2*
Was the CV produced using a standard software package?	Yes 1 No 0	SCORE *1*
Was it easy to print?	Yes 1 No 0	SCORE *1*
Is it well typed?	Yes 1 No 0	SCORE *1*

Is the typeface suitable?	Yes 1 No 0 SCORE *1*

B Accuracy

Does the CV have any spelling mistakes?	Yes 0 No 3 SCORE *0*
Is it written in the third person singular?	Yes 2 No 0 SCORE *0*
Does it include any clichés, jargon or slang?	Yes 0 No 1 SCORE *0*
Are all the sentences constructed correctly?	Yes 1 No 0 SCORE *1*
Are they punctuated correctly?	Yes 1 No 0 SCORE *0*
Do they include active words?	Yes 6 No 0 SCORE *0*
Does the CV clarify abbreviations?	Yes 1 No 0 SCORE *1*
Does it repeat words, facts, or thoughts?	Yes 0 No 1 SCORE *0*

C Content

Is your preferred name used?	Yes 1 No 0 SCORE *1*

Does the CV include full postal address, telephone number and email address?	Yes 1 No 0	SCORE *0*
Does the CV include any irrelevant information, such as:		
Place of birth	Yes 0 No 1	SCORE *1*
Children's names and ages	Yes 0 No 1	SCORE *1*
Spouse's name	Yes 0 No 1	SCORE *1*
Referees	Yes 0 No 1	SCORE *1*
Religion	Yes 0 No 1	SCORE *1*
Hobbies	Yes 0 No 1	SCORE *0*
Salary/benefits	Yes 0 No 1	SCORE *0*
Is sufficient educational detail included?	Yes 2 No 0	SCORE *0*
Is a covering letter included with the CV for this analysis test?	Yes 2 No 0	SCORE *0*
Does the CV cover all important facts?	Yes 6 No 0	SCORE *0*

D Effectiveness

Is the CV geared towards a job target or field of work?	Yes 6 No 0	SCORE *6*
Does the CV emphasize your relevant skills?	Yes 5 No 0	SCORE *0*
Is the CV selling you? Does it stress accomplishments over skills and duties?	Yes 5 No 0	SCORE *0*
Is the CV written in the employer's language?	Yes 1 No 0	SCORE *0*
Does the CV show that you have thought carefully about the job before applying for it?	Yes 1 No 0	SCORE *0*
Does the CV demonstrate how the employer will benefit from taking you on?	Yes 1 No 0	SCORE *0*
Is the CV exciting to read?	Yes 1 No 0	SCORE *0*

E Style and Personality

Does the CV reflect your personality well?	Yes 6 No 0	SCORE *0*
Does the CV emphasize your job responsibilities?	Yes 6 No 0	SCORE *0*

Does the CV show that you have researched the company and job?	**Yes 1 No 0** **SCORE** *0*
Does the CV reflect a positive image of you?	**Yes 5 No 0** **SCORE** *0*
Does the CV show that you enjoy work and life?	**Yes 1 No 0** **SCORE 1**

SCORING

	Maximum Score	Your Score
Presentation and Layout	26	*12*
Accuracy	16	*2*
Content	19	*6*
Effectiveness	20	*6*
Style and Personality	19	*1*
Total	100	***27***

RATING

This is a WEAK CV.

THREE

Targeting your CV

This chapter is the crux of writing a perfect CV. You cannot produce a good and effective CV without ensuring that it is targeted towards the job in question. A targeted CV shouts loud and clear 'This is what I can offer your company' and the effect is very powerful.

Targeting is something which most people avoid, skip over or make a half-attempt at by just slapping the words 'Job target is a position as a....' across the top of the front page of the CV. There is much more to it than this. Targeting is quite a complex and in-depth process, which requires a reasonable amount of time, effort and thought. This chapter will lead you through it step by step.

Most CVs do not gear the information contained in them towards the particular reader. Having completed the analysis test in Chapter 2, you may now be aware that your own CV cannot be classified as a 'targeted CV'.

Benefits of targeting

By targeting your CV to a particular job, you will:

☑ **Make yourself stand out from the competition**. There is obviously more to you than your ability to write and type a CV, upload it to numerous job-boards and apply to every job that you see advertised on the Internet and in the press..

- ☑ **Focus on your job campaign**. You will know what job you are looking for and therefore will not waste time applying for jobs that don't suit you. This will minimize the risk of your making any disastrous decisions or career moves.
- ☑ **Be active in your approach to job hunting.** The key to successful job hunting is to keep at it even if it takes some time. It is much better to spend a bit of time each day than to devote one whole day a month to it. Remember that securing the right job can take anything from a few months to as long as two years; bearing this in mind can prevent you from becoming disheartened. Targeting will also show you that it is not necessary to resort to gimmicky tricks or brash approaches in order to attract an employer's attention (they don't work anyway).
- ☑ **Maintain a positive attitude.** Once you know what job you are looking for, it is much easier to find. Working through the process of choosing your job targets will help you to realize your potential and give your self-confidence a boost. Having a positive attitude and self-belief can then be reflected in the tone of your CV. If you value yourself, others will value you too. A positive attitude will also stand you in good stead for the path ahead.
- ☑ **Take ownership of your career.** It is your job, your career and your life, so you must be the one in the driving seat. If you want something, it is up to you to achieve it: too many people fall into the categories of 'would like to be', 'want to be' or 'cannot be'. If you want to avoid these pitfalls, take control of your future now and direct it the way you want it to go, because no one is going to do this for you – not even your current boss or employer. Place ownership of your career with you rather than with your employer, who in any case is far more concerned with his/her own career than with yours.
- ☑ **Arouse the employer's interest.** An employer is far more likely to interview and offer a job to someone who shows an interest in his/her company than to someone who simply attaches their CV to an email and sends it in.

One of my contacts told me quite openly that she had a full head count in her department when she received a targeted CV and a speculative covering letter through the post. This CV was one of the best she had seen in her 14 years of recruiting financial managers. What fascinated her about it was that the person had identified clearly the type of position he was looking for and highlighted their immense experience. She was so impressed with the CV that she interviewed the person and made a case to the personnel department to appoint him in a new role. She did so because she knew that this calibre of person was hard to come by.

Targeting is thus immensely powerful and it is relatively easy to achieve. Best of all, the benefits are all yours.

Importance of targeting

The first thing to remember is that most applicants don't make use of a targeted CV because they don't know *how to do it*. Due to this, most people adopt a very passive approach to job hunting, with no clear idea of the job they are looking for. Many job seekers look for an 'interesting' or 'challenging' job or one that offers them 'opportunities' – whatever that means. I recently asked an undergraduate what line of work he would be going into when he graduated and the reply was 'management'. When I asked what he meant by management, he told me that it was the management of people. I'd heard enough: enough to realize that I hadn't a clue what he was looking for and it appeared that neither did he!

People often think that they are broadening their chances if they express a willingness to do anything and everything. However, it doesn't work this way. Employers want to see that you have a *clear idea* of what you want to do, because it matters to their business. The employer is concerned that you are the right person for the job on offer. Whether or not the job is 'challenging' or 'interesting' is an interesting challenge for you!

Basic principles of formulating job targets

You, and only you, can decide what job you want to do. However, listed below are the basic principles of targeting to help make your decisions a little bit easier.

1. Your profession

A profession is what you do for a living, what you have spent time training to do, or what you want to be doing. Everyone has a profession, but this does not necessarily mean that this is the job they currently do each day. For example, they may be doing temporary work, be unemployed, be off work sick, be retraining, or be having a career break. So, remember that just because you may not be doing the job you are trained to do, you still have your profession.

What is your profession?

You have probably been asked this question hundreds of times before. You need a succinct answer, and, to help you to arrive at that, think about what you put down on a passport application form. What do you tell people when you are asked this question while on holiday and don't want to bore them with the in-depth details of your work? Do you say that you are a secretary, a nurse, a teacher, an accountant, a retailer, a banker, an insurance worker, an engineer, a consultant, a designer, a tax inspector, a production worker, a marketeer, a salesman, a buyer, a quantity surveyor, a researcher, a farmer, an artist, a hairdresser, a computer analyst…?

When asked what they do for a living, people often talk about 'being in' something. They might say that they are in marketing, publishing or the media. However, 'being in' something is not the same as having a profession. It may sound impressive, but it has very little to do with what the person does each day, their role, their input and output, their future and potential. This answer relies solely upon the glamour of the profession itself. A better answer would be 'I am a marketeer', and then to go on to explain the core features of the product you market and the company you work for.

Your primary concern

Your primary concern when searching for work is to look for a job which is relevant or applicable to your profession. Why? Because it is the primary concern of the employer to have someone who can actually do the job on offer, and what better insurance policy is there than to find someone who is either doing the same job elsewhere or has done this type of work before? So if an employer is looking to recruit a retail manager, he will want a retail manager, not a salesman wanting to become a retail manager.

The first basic principle of job targeting is, therefore, that a job target must relate closely to what you do or have done in your previous jobs or educational training. In fact, the closer your targeted job relates to your current job and experience, the higher your salary expectation can be.

2. The field

The field or speciality of work is often confused with the profession. People often refer more to their field of work than to their profession itself. To assist you in making the distinction, note that:

Selling is a profession	*but* insurance is the field.
Teaching is a profession	*but* primary school age is the field.
Design is a profession	*but* interior design is the field.
Civil engineering is a profession	*but* public health is the field. *but* road construction is the field
Accountancy is a profession	*but* taxation is the field. *but* credit control is the field.

Thus, in simplistic terms, the field is the speciality of the profession, the bit that makes you ***you***, and different from the competition. The field is therefore an indication of a person's experience. Someone could be classed as very experienced if they have spent a number of years or even decades in one specialist field, or if they have been successful in a number of different fields within their profession. Bear in mind that the longer a person stays in a particular field the more likely it is that he/she will be typecast in that job and therefore will not be considered for other roles. Of course, this is not a problem if his/her future is always going to be in, say, credit control rather than accountancy. One advantage of specialism of this sort is that there are often fewer people with the same level of experience, so higher salaries can be demanded or earned. The disadvantage could be that the person sacrifices flexibility, and employers might interpret the fact that he/she has spent so long in a particular field to mean that he/she can't do anything different.

The other major danger could be that your chosen field is suddenly threatened by changes in business practices or the wider environment. For example, fields such as being a tracer/draughtsman in the engineering profession are threatened by the introduction of CAD/CAM computer systems, while the field of defence engineering within mechanical engineering is threatened by the diminishing defence industry and the increased domination of electronic engineering.

Glamour versus job satisfaction

Some fields are more attractive than others, but this doesn't necessarily mean that the jobs are any better. In fact, it sometimes means the opposite: because the demand for jobs is higher in glamour fields such as broadcasting, public relations (PR) and advertising, companies can often get away with offering lower salaries than in other fields.

Some people also become so blinded by their chosen glamour field that they forego opportunities which exist in other fields and take a job simply because it is glamorous. For example, a person's profession may be a caterer, but a glamour field to be in is the theatre, so they take a job selling ice creams in the interval and forego a more lucrative and equally, if not more, rewarding job in another sector. Remember it is the job and not the field that determines job satisfaction.

3. Salary

For most people, money is an important issue because they need and rely upon it. If money isn't important to you, you either have family money, have won the lottery or have worked out ways to live without it. If this is the case, keep this information to yourself or you may risk putting off would-be employers.

Whether you like it or not, money and the power of money is a great way in which employers can control, influence and in some cases threaten you. Employers often use money to control their employees, so if you show or imply that money doesn't matter to you, you could wave goodbye to the job on offer.

Because of this, your job target must include a salary figure which determines your market rate, covers your basic living expenses and allows you room for enjoyment.

4. The company

A job target should also include the kind of company you want to work for, although try to avoid setting your sights on certain companies as the competition will inevitably be strong. Equally, don't eliminate other companies simply because you don't like what you have heard: it might not be true, and in any case someone else's opinion may not be the same as yours.

The following list will give you an idea of the sorts of options open to you and will help you to decide where and for whom you want to work.

- **A large national or multinational limited or public company.** This is a company where you will be a small cog in a large machine – a company often governed by rules, regulations, the past or someone else (head office or the shareholders) where your influence may be minimal and limited. Career advancement may also mean relocation, perhaps even several times.
- **A smaller, locally headquartered company**. Here you may have a greater say, but less opportunity for advancement and change.

- **A family-owned company or partnership.** This is a company normally run on tradition, hopes and dreams. If your job is in a 'niche' role it is often a good place to work, but family companies can be claustrophobic and if you are not a family member or 'in' with the family it can be restricting.
- **A company known for its social conscience.** Here the company's philosophies and attitudes tend to be reflected in the working environment. If you follow these philosophies you will be fine; if not stay away, as you could find it intimidating.
- **A company where your involvement would be minimal.** Here you can clock in at 9am and leave at 5pm. Your work life won't encroach on your leisure time.
- **A company where your involvement would be great.** You may even have a chance to become a star. Here it is taken for granted that you will leave only when the job is done, regardless of the time.
- **A company which is highly competitive.** This sort of company will offer you the opportunity for career advancement.
- **A company which is not competitive.** This company offers instead stability and consistency.

Take your pick and approach those companies that appeal to you.

5. The job

The job itself is its title, salary, duties, the level of responsibility and the amount of satisfaction you would gain from it.

Don't fall into the trap of building your job target around a single job title, as this is too specific and limiting. In any case, the same title doesn't mean the same thing to every company, as each will lump together different roles and functions and call jobs different things. Also, try not to think about the detail of the job: for example, the number of people who will report to you, your desk, and the type of company car. These things change constantly and can always be negotiated at an interview if you are disappointed with some aspect.

6. Your current employment status

Your current employment status affects your position. It determines how much power you have to negotiate with the employer and might give you reason to change your requirements. For example, you may have set a desired salary of £43,000, but if you have been out of work for a while and a job is offered at £39,000 it is advisable to accept it. Thus, your requirements will change and you must recognize this and change your job search accordingly. A job target should not be fixed.

7. Your special requirements

It is your career, so if you have special requirements try to incorporate this into your job campaign. For example, your hobbies may mean that you prefer flexible working hours; you may prefer to spend as little time as possible commuting; or you may prefer to work for a recognized company name. If something is important to you, include it in your job search.

Committing your job targets to paper

To work out your job target/s, fill in the gaps in Figure 1 on page 59. When you have done this, you will be able to produce a job target similar to the example in Figure 2.

Changing your profession

The section on 'Your profession' above may have convinced you that you want to change it, perhaps because you are unhappy or dissatisfied with your current one. In fact, there are a whole number of reasons why people want to change their professions. Try to identify your reason from the questions below:

- Have you only ever had a job before and not a profession?
- Have you outgrown your current profession, so that it no longer gives you the same spark as it once did?
- Have you reached your potential in this profession and can no longer climb any higher within it?
- Have your circumstances changed so that you can no longer commit yourself to your profession in the same way as before?
- Do you just want to start over again?
- Do you just need a new challenge?

The thing to remember is that in the majority of cases it is never too late to change. Note that I have said majority, because in some circumstances age, sex and experience are barriers to entry into certain professions. You will need to find out whether your desired new profession is open or closed to you by doing some research. Talk to people within the profession itself and to the appropriate institutions. Careers libraries and books will give you information on who to contact and where to write to for help. When writing or talking to these people, always provide details of your work experience to date, educational background and future career aspirations. They will be able to advise you and confirm whether or not your new career plan/profession is a realistic possibility. With this knowledge, you will be able to decide whether or not you still want to make the change, and if the effort required to bring it about is worth it. Figure 3 summarizes the stages involved.

Although in most cases it is possible to change profession, it is not normally particularly easy. It is often a lengthy process, because the change has to be made in a number of steps and stages which will bridge the gap from your current to your desired profession.

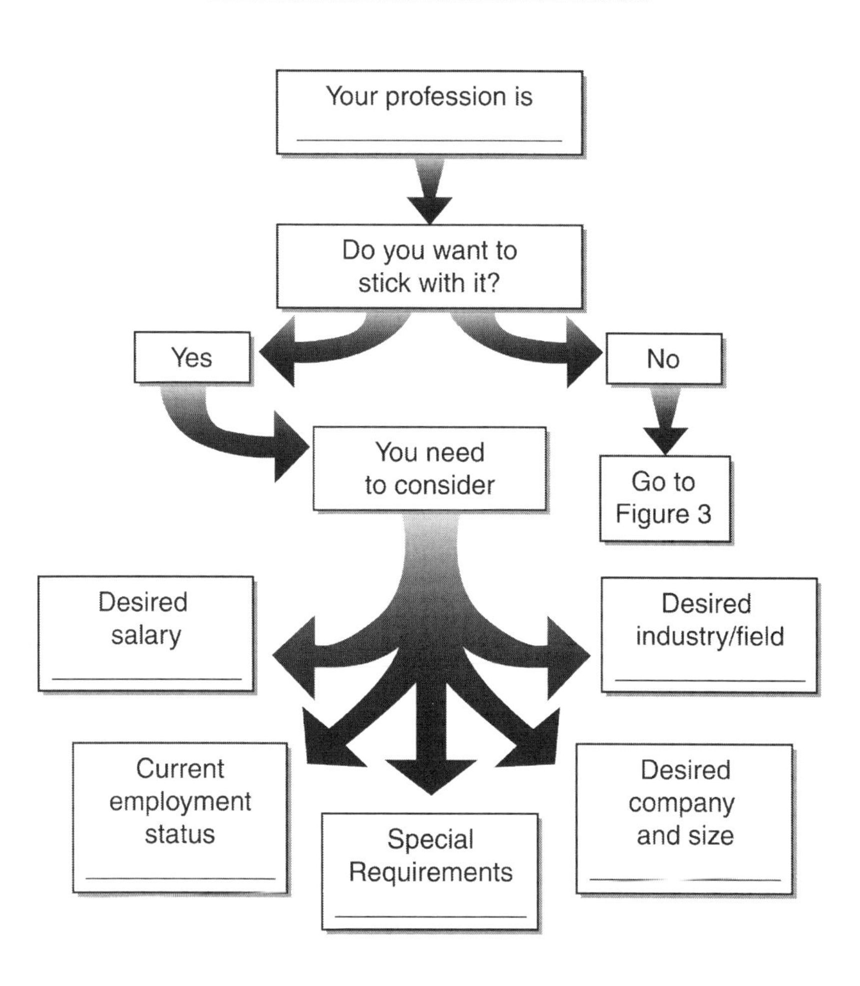
Working out
your job targets
Your profession is
Do you want to
stick with it?
Yes
No
You need
to consider
Go to
Figure 3
Desired
salary
Desired
industry/field
Current
employment
status
Special
Requirements
Desired
company
and size

Figure 1

Example of a job target

Profession
Marketing

Field
Branded consumer goods

Company
Large company with opportunities and advancement

Salary
At least £45,000

Special requirements
Working flexible hours, company car, private health care and company pension

Current employment status
Full-time employment, no hurry to move and looking for something over the next year

Figure 2

Changing your profession

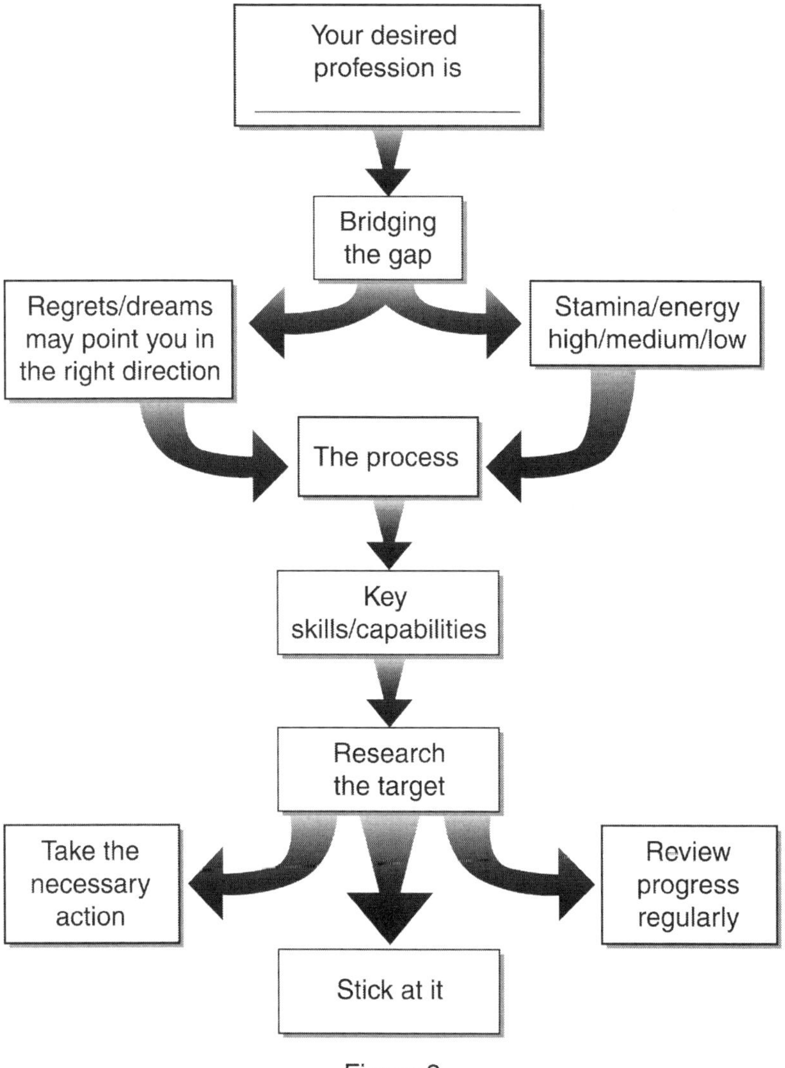

Figure 3

BRIDGE FIELDS

The easiest and safest option is to change your field of work in order to bridge the gap between the two professions. The new field is called the 'bridge field'.

For example, one of my clients was an accountant. He had become bored with his job and he desperately needed a change. He had always yearned to be a solicitor, and when he met me he was feeling some sense of regret and disappointment that he had not become one. However, as he was sure that this was the direction he wanted to pursue and research showed that it was a genuine possibility, we worked upon bridging the gap between these two professions. We had to do this because it would have been too radical a change to go straight from being an accountant to being a solicitor. Employers would *never* have bought into this sudden change of direction, and my client would almost certainly have been rejected from every job that he applied for as a solicitor. This is because there would have been too many uncertainties for the employer, who would have felt that my client had no proven track record or ability, no understanding and no working knowledge of being a solicitor.

The route my client took to bridge the gap was to join a solicitor's firm in a position where he advised and helped on the financial side of cases while studying part-time, one day per week, for the necessary exams. The process took between four and five years, but he was finally appointed as a solicitor. Figure 4 maps out the steps taken.

FULL-TIME STUDY

The other method that some people use to bridge the gap is to give up their job and embark on a full-time study course. With this method you will lose your earnings, but still incur all the costs of training and your living expenses. You therefore run the

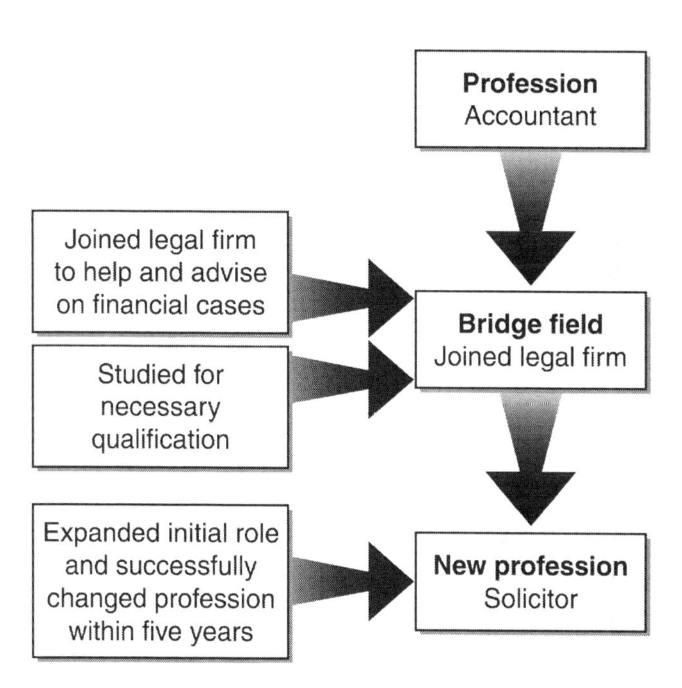
Bridging the gap
Profession
Accountant
Joined legal firm to help and advise on financial cases
Bridge field
Joined legal firm
Studied for necessary qualification
Expanded initial role and successfully changed profession within five years
New profession
Solicitor

Figure 4

risk of amassing huge debts, because you may not qualify for a grant to cover some of your expenses. I recently heard of someone who was going to study to do an MBA (Master of Business Administration).

The cost of the course in terms of loss of earnings, training and living expenses was £45,000 over 18 months. This person obviously considered the benefit to be worth his while. I hope he is right!

The major risk factors with this method are that you may not actually like the course/profession, by which time it is too late, and that you will be out of the workforce for a long period of time. Although you will re-enter with technical expertise you will have little or no practical experience, and employers may not find this all that attractive. Before you embark on such a course, sound out employers to see how they view such a method of retraining.

If, however, you have the funds and are having a career break or a year off work, this method of learning may be perfect for you.

You have to know in your heart that this profession is what you truly want to be doing day in day out. As long as you know this, and are totally committed and stick at it, you will achieve your dream job/profession. Most people don't, because they either lose sight of their vision or give up when the going gets tough. And it will be tough – because employers want committed employees, not faint- or half-hearted ones.

A balanced CV

Having read this chapter, you should now be familiar with the concept of targeting and, more importantly, know how to create your own job targets. These will give your job search campaign a structure that it wouldn't otherwise have. Start with your profession, add your salary and pick a field you want to be in, but above all be open-minded and stay flexible.

The results of this chapter will now form the central thread and tone of your CV. However, you should aim for a balance between being too broad and too specific, and avoid the following types of targeting:

- **The targeted-wide CV.** This is the CV that covers anything and everything and is advertised in the newspaper and on the Internet (in France CVs have even been placed on wine bottles) in the vain hope that someone, somewhere might happen to see it. Even if someone does, why should they react?

- **The intrusive targeted CV and covering letter.** The applicant offends the employer by bragging about him/herself, making unrealistic promises of help or twisting information he/she has heard on the grapevine. For example, the applicant may write that he/she has heard that the company is in financial trouble or is in the process of restructuring – the company will know this but may not want you to know it or make unsolicited offers of help. Beware of this approach: it is taking targeting too far.

FOUR

Qualifications

This chapter will explain the importance of qualifications, how to present them, and what to do if you don't have the right qualifications for the job on offer.

Importance of qualifications

Qualifications are crucial to job applications and the job market. They are normally the first bit the employer turns to when he reads a CV. Qualifications represent what you have done in life, rather than what you think you can do or what you hope to do in the future; they are your track record and it is up to you to shout about them.

Employers love qualifications because they are the only insurance policy they have. Recruitment is a difficult, lengthy and expensive process and there is no way of being right all the time. When an employee doesn't fulfil expectations, the most obvious question is 'Who hired him/her?' Fingers are pointed, egos get bruised and promotions can be postponed due to bad recruitment decisions. However, if the employee looked good on paper then the person who hired him/her can always be let off the hook. Hence, employers still cling to qualifications, because this means they are not making decisions based upon intangibles. The importance of qualifications does vary from company to company, the general rule being that the more bureaucratic a company is the greater the importance placed on qualifications.

Some companies are so adamant about the skills required that they make all candidates take certain tests to reveal both their depth of knowledge and their personality. However, some candidates have taken so many of these tests before that they can actually present themselves in the way the company wants them to be, rather than as they actually are! Other companies, if they are impressed with a candidate, will waive a special qualification requirement on the understanding that he/she undergoes some kind of training. In addition, smaller companies are often more loosely structured and can afford a flexible qualification policy.

Qualifications are vital to the employment decision, so you must not keep your assets a secret. And don't downplay virtues such as accuracy, loyalty and dependability, as these are qualities that could swing the balance in your favour.

Education, experience and personality

Advertisements highlight the desired qualifications that the company is looking for. Most people assume that 'qualifications' refer to educational achievements – the grades achieved in and recorded on certificates that can be waved under the employer's nose as proof of ability. However, there is far more to qualifications than examination records: hence the successful business entrepreneur who claims proudly that he left school without a single qualification.

Too many candidates reject themselves from the selection process because they don't feel that they meet the qualification requirements. If you view qualifications as purely educational you will reduce substantially the number of options available to you, but on the whole employers are looking for more than just 'educational' qualifications. They also want job-related qualifications, which refer to your background, skills gained and the companies you have worked for. The other qualification is your personality, which determines your character, how you come across and how much potential you have. This is the bit that can give you the edge over another candidate with similar expertise and experience as yourself, so don't downplay its importance. Remember: if you don't include it in your CV, it will be assumed that you don't have a personality.

If you look at job advertisements you will see that employers usually split qualifications into these three sectors. Listed below are examples of qualification requirements that might appear under each heading.

EDUCATIONAL QUALIFICATIONS

- Education to 'A' Level.
- Degree essential (a 2:1 degree or an MBA).
- Professional qualification (CIPD, ICE, CIMA, ICAEW).
- Good business knowledge of a foreign language an advantage.

JOB/LIFE QUALIFICATIONS

- Preferably a minimum of (states number) years' experience in (states the technical speciality, for example, retail management, teaching, computing, accountancy, sales and purchasing).
- Experience of working for a multinational, blue chip company.
- Experience of strategic planning and of driving plans to fruition.
- Successful track record (see Chapter 7).
- Driving licence essential.
- Practical experience essential.
- Include a list of all courses attended.

PERSONALITY

- Good Communicator, both verbally and on paper.
- 'Hands on' approach.
- Inspirational and entrepreneurial leader able to build trust and respect, both internally and externally.
- Outgoing personality with a clear understanding of bottom-line performance.
- High level of interpersonal skills to liaise with all levels of staff and immediately gain peer support.
- Independent person with the business judgement and financial awareness to channel your effort and the company's resources effectively and profitably.

The chosen candidate will be the person who scores high in all three areas, so don't count yourself out if you are stronger in one area than another. It is the overall picture that matters.

If you do not have the required qualifications

How do you get over the hurdle of not having the exact qualifications for which the advertisement asks? You may think it is a waste of time to apply for a job unless you have all the qualifications stated in the advertisement; however, this is not always the case, because qualifications can be broken down into essential and desirable. For example, the advertisement may state 'an absolute minimum of five years' experience', which is quite a vague requirement, as are terms such as 'extensive experience'. In these circumstances, give yourself the benefit of the doubt and you will often get an interview if your background is reasonably close to the requirements.

On the other hand, the advertisement may be much more specific than this and state that something is absolutely essential. If you don't have the qualifications but feel you have the ability to do the job, be honest in your CV, then highlight the disadvantage in the covering letter but stress your abilities (see Chapter 10).

If you have been out of the workforce for a period of time, you may be less confident about your abilities and perhaps your lack of work experience. However, try not to get caught up in what you don't have – remember above all what you do have to offer the employer.

For example, an advertisement may demand 'at least two years' fundraising experience: you may have been at home raising the children and been involved with a local fundraising charity for one year. The key is not to exaggerate what you did to make it sound more impressive, but to sell what you did. It is better in this situation to say something along the lines of 'In the year that I worked on the fundraising committee revenue increased by 75 per cent', than to say 'I know that I have the ability to fundraise successfully'. The first statement adds value whereas the second is just your opinion.

The thing to remember with qualifications is that the gap may not be as wide as you think, so it is often worth a try and you will never know until you actually do. The rule is never to build your hopes up too high; there are no guarantees, but if you keep trying before long you will be invited to attend an interview.

Your chances are very slim if your background doesn't meet the specifications *at all*. It is best to accept this and spend your time applying for more suitable jobs, or retraining for your desired job target/profession. Otherwise, you will go on receiving rejection letter after rejection letter, and this can be very demoralizing.

NEVER LIE ABOUT QUALIFICATIONS

Never lie about your qualifications. Apart from it being illegal and immoral to do so, they are the easiest things to check up on. An employer once told me that he interviewed a man who had put on his CV that he had a degree from Oxford University. 'I too had been to Oxford, so naturally I was interested to find out which College he had been to.' 'Oh no, not Oxford University, England,' the candidate laughed,' Oxford University is a little place off the Ganges.' 'Not quite what I was looking for,' smiled my friend.

If you lie, you are almost certain to slip up somewhere. Perhaps you will get caught out at the interview, or promote yourself into a job you can't cope with. If you do get found out, you are likely to be fired on the spot and, like everything illegal, it will be recorded somewhere and you will have to face the consequences for the rest of your working life. Falsification is therefore simply not worth the risk.

Marketing your qualifications

Most people either can't or are not used to marketing their qualifications, but it is up to you to evaluate yourself and to present yourself on the basis of this evaluation. The key is to put *all* your marketable skills down on paper. The sections below will show you how to do a self-inventory, and how to portray your strengths and be aware of your weaknesses. Work experience is covered in Chapter 5. Remember, though, that it is not necessary to be per cent perfect in order to make a favourable impression upon an employer.

A typical CV will follow this format:

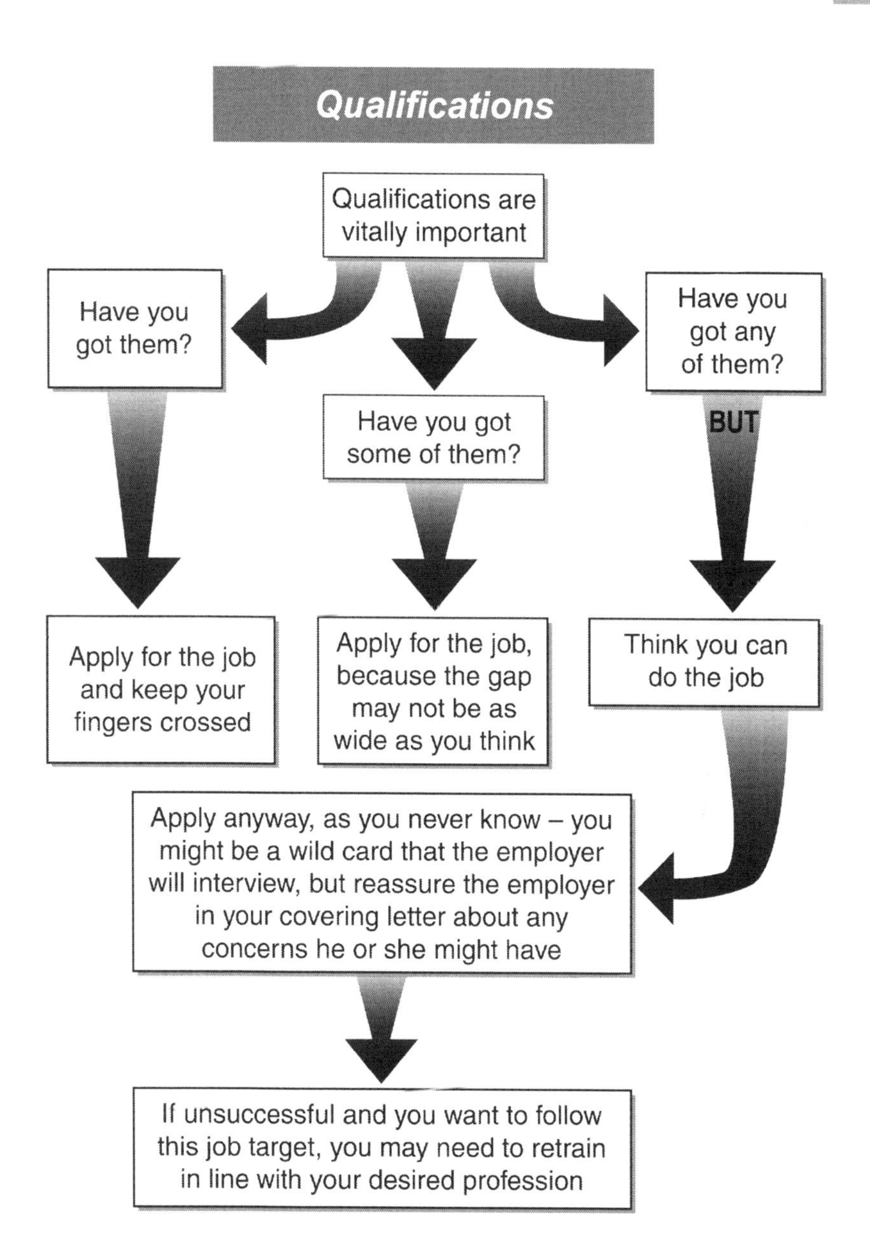
Qualifications
Qualifications are vitally important
Have you got them?
Have you got some of them?
Have you got any of them?
BUT
Apply for the job and keep your fingers crossed
Apply for the job, because the gap may not be as wide as you think
Think you can do the job
Apply anyway, as you never know – you might be a wild card that the employer will interview, but reassure the employer in your covering letter about any concerns he or she might have
If unsuccessful and you want to follow this job target, you may need to retrain in line with your desired profession

Figure 5

Page 1: The selling page
Personal details
Capabilities

Page 2: The track record page
Education
Work experience (including jobs done, duties, achievements and companies worked for)

EDUCATION AND TRAINING

The education section of the CV should generally be placed after personal details and capabilities sections and is therefore normally at the top of the second page. However, if this is your first job the education section is the key to your abilities, so it should be placed at the bottom of the first page. If your education is not all that spectacular, place it after the work experience section.

The summary of your education must be accurate, brief and easy to follow. Start with the highest level first. Indicate the level of the subject (professional status, degree, including perhaps the subjects you majored in, and 'GCSE/O' and 'A' Levels), the establishment you attended, and the dates you achieved your qualifications. Mention also any prizes or awards won, or any positions of responsibility you held, but don't elaborate – the employer can ask you about this at the interview.

Do not include any business training or courses attended under the education section, as it will become cluttered and messy. The place for these is in the work experience section under achievements. In this section, instead of giving a long and boring list of every course you have ever been on, include only those that are relevant to the job target and say why, and explain what you learnt. This will show that you didn't sleep your way through the course!

If you speak a foreign language it is worth including this under the education section, usually at the end.

The finished education section should look something like this:

Education

Member of ________________ Institution, 19__

BA (Hons) (2:1) Subjects/s, University/College, 19__

'A' Levels, Subject (grade), Subject (grade), Subject (grade), College/School name, town and county, 19__

GCSEs/'O' levels, Subjects (grades), College/School name, town and county, 19__

Positions of responsibility include: examples such as form captain and school prefect

Fluent in spoken (language), and achieved (grade) in the written paper

PERSONALITY

Demonstrating your personality in the CV will increase your attractiveness as a candidate. Employers like to interview all candidates and 90 per cent of the final decision is based upon the candidate's personality. On their own, virtues such as being positive, influential, communicative, dependable and logical may not get you a job, but you could be eliminated from the selection process if you appear to lack any of them. So, if you reflect your personality in the CV you will stop being a 'faceless' candidate and will give yourself an advantage over the competition.

How do you make yourself seem special? When presenting your personality on paper you need to do more than just copy out verbatim the qualities that are listed in the advertisement: employers find nothing more irritating than rereading their own advertisement time after time. Anyone can copy, and anyone can claim that they are 'a loyal team player and a good communicator'. What employers want is for you to conjure up a picture of yourself. The personality inventory will give you an idea of the volume and types of details to include.

Your personality inventory

The personality profile should be placed subtly in the capabilities section on the first page of the CV (see sample CVs in Chapter 9). You will need five or six examples to give the employer a true taste of your personal qualities. Remember that nobody finds it easy to write about themselves, but now is no time to be shy. Shed your embarrassment and concentrate on making yourself look a winner. You may have forgotten just what an asset you are!

Create a positive image of yourself by choosing words that reflect something about you as a person. Avoid non-descriptive, woolly words such as 'involved' and 'responsible', which leave the reader none the wiser about your input and activities. Avoid also the throwaway words such as 'reasonable' communicator, which only raise doubt in the mind of the employer. Choose instead the active words listed below or ones of you own.

Below is a list of words to help you determine what you have to offer. Read each word, pause and think about it. Ask yourself if this word describes you. If it does, tick it. Once you have completed this exercise, circle the five words that are most like you and cross out the five that are least like you. Remember that there are no right or wrong answers. The words you have circled can now be used to set the tone of your CV.

Words for your personality inventory

Accurate	Direct	Inquisitive	Probing
Alert	Driving	Kind	Quiet
Amiable	Eager	Logical	Reflective
Anxious	Factual	Mild	Reserved
Assertive	Firm	Mobile	Restless
Careful	Forceful	Modest	Self-starter
Cautious	Friendly	Non-demanding	Steady
Communicative	Good listener	Optimistic	Serious
Competitive	Good with words	Perfectionist	Strong-willed
Compliant	Impatient	Persistent	Stubborn
Conservative	Independent	Persuasive	Sympathetic
Deliberate	Influential	Positive	Systematic
Dependable		Precise	Unpretentious

Presenting your personality qualities

Above all, you must present your qualities in the context of what you think your would-be employer needs. This is the basic work principle. It is not so much what you have going for you that will get you a job, but your ability to convince the would-be employer that what you have is what he needs. In other words, you need to fulfil the employer's need.

Start with the job advertisement. Read it thoroughly and if necessary write it out. Underline the personality qualifications listed. Now refer to your words list. If you haven't included some of the employer's stipulations, you must; otherwise, you are immediately putting yourself at a disadvantage. Remember also that you are doing yourself no favours if you include negative or flippant statements.

Employers tend to look for the same or similar types of personal qualities. The most popular are:

- Good communication skills.
- Ability to handle pressure.

- Ability to take the initiative.
- Dependability.

To present these in marketable terms you need to answer how, where and when you use or demonstrate these qualities, thereby turning a straightforward statement into one which has meaning and power. So, instead of saying 'I am dependable, communicative and able to work under pressure', you could fulfil the employer's need by including under the capabilities section:

- Developing business relationships with colleagues and supervisors based on mutual respect and trust. (Communication)
- Meeting deadlines and handling pressure in a fast-moving, dynamic environment. Leaving work when the job is done regardless of the time. (Pressure)
- Improving personal and technical skills through courses, self-study and dedication. (Initiative)
- Getting to the heart of problems by focusing on critical information and performing the work with minimal supervision. (Dependability)

When writing about your personal qualities, always be honest with yourself. For example, you may think that you can cope with pressure, but the pressure of this job may be different to your idea of it. If you are honest in the CV, then at the interview you can decide whether this job and its pressure is really something that you would thrive on or just hate. Focus on your strengths and be positive in writing, and this will be communicated to the reader – positive people are an asset to any organization, and it will just be a matter of time before you reap what you have sown!

FIVE

Work Experience

The work experience section is the third and last part of the qualification record. Your work experience indicates your suitability for the job, which is judged on:

- Whether your background in terms of your previous companies' size, function, turnover, profitability, ownership and product/service is compatible with that of the would-be company.
- Whcther your role and duties in your previous posts are in line with the job on offer.
- Whether you achieved within your role, or just did the job and collected your salary at the end of each month (see Chapter 7).

When you join a company it is similar to entering into a marriage. The strength of your affiliation and compatibility will depend on how much time and effort you put into your research of the prospective company; otherwise, it may appear that you are not serious and are only looking for a transitory post. Employers are not necessarily looking to employ you for life or for better or worse, but they are looking for compatibility, commitment and contribution.

Most people have a reasonable idea of what their current company does, but usually omit this vital information in the CV. It is almost as if they expect the prospective employer to be aware of what every company in the country produces. However, I have come across people who, after a bit of questioning, admit that they literally have no idea what their company does or produces. This is almost unbelievable – in one case the employee had been with the company for five years!

So, when you write your CV you need to set the company scene, explain what you did, indicate how well you did it and tailor the information towards the prospective company.

Exceptions

THE NEW STARTER

You may be a school-leaver, or college or university graduate without much work experience. That is fine, because no-one expects you to have much experience when you are young. However, employers do expect the young to have ambition, a willingness to learn, energy, drive and, above all, enthusiasm. Don't try to compensate for lack of experience in the CV by overplaying your theoretical knowledge, because it really is OK to be green – and this is almost the only time in your working life that you can get away with it!

Under the work experience section in the CV include anything and everything that you have done, for example, holiday jobs, travel experience, working on the school magazine or involvement with societies. Handle the latter as if it were a job, giving your title, the club/society name and a brief description of your role and achievements.

THE INTERNAL APPLICANT

The internal applicant cannot get away with handing in a poor and sloppy application just because he/she already works for the company. High standards apply to all candidates. Remember, too, that it does your image no good to submit a substandard application, as it will be held on your file. Put as much effort into applying for an internal job as an external one.

ONE-COMPANY RECORD

Having worked for only one company is not a problem. Show the name of the company at the top and list all the jobs you have held chronologically, with the most recent first (see sample CV in Chapter 9). It is advisable to demonstrate some degree of flexibility rather than give the prospective employer the impression that you took a job 20 years ago and have become 'stuck' in it!

RETURNERS TO WORK

Returners to work make up a huge proportion of the job market. If you can market your qualities and skills in the right way you will stand as good a chance as any job hunter, especially as you have all your life experiences to draw upon. Don't accept a second rate, lowly paid, mediocre position, because there is no reason why you should. Value yourself and employers will value you too, for you have lived, may have done voluntary work and experienced many different things in the time that you were out of work. Use all this to your advantage.

When compiling your work experience record, avoid a huge gap which makes it look as if you last worked for a company 15 years ago and have done nothing else since. Equally, avoid putting that for 15 years you were a housewife/mother or having a career break! Instead, sell your skills and yourself into the job you are after, because much of what you have done at home is applicable to your work ambitions. If you feel that your skills need brushing up you could always consider a short course in the relevant subject.

Above all, you must show that your CV is continuous, that you have had recent experience and that you are up-to-date with working practices. For example, you may be looking for a job in media/PR, perhaps with a local newspaper or in a company's marketing department. So, you could include experience gained on local committees and write:

1989 – 2006 **Freelance voluntary work (while raising the family). Worked on various committees for local charities, schools and local societies, Swindon, Wiltshire.**

Responsible for cold calling local press, writing press releases and co-ordinating local advertising campaign for the National Childbirth Trust (NCT) with a limited budget. (You don't have to state the number of hours you put in or if you were paid. What counts more is that you were active and not vegetative in your period away from work.)

The NCT is a national charity set up in 1946 throughout England. Scotland, Wales and Northern Ireland. On a national level, the charity works to influence government and health service breastfeeding and early parenthood. On a local level, it provides support antenatally with classes and postnatally through a range of activities. (It is helpful to give a few background details about the organization.)

Major Achievements:

Increased local support and awareness of the NCT: number of people attending major fundraising day increased by 50 per cent in the two years while a committee member. (And so on, including anything and everything that is relevant to your job target.)

Get rid of any tendencies towards insecurity and make your experiences work for you.

Work experience inventory

Think carefully about your work experience and then fill in the form below. Don't just make a rushed attempt: most job hunters do this, so here is your chance to get a competitive advantage.

Current Employer ______________________

Location ______________________

From ________ To ________

Job Title ______________________

Previous Employer ______________________

Location ______________________

From ________ To ________

Job Title ______________________

Repeat the Previous Employer details as necessary, depending on how many you have worked for.

POINTS TO NOTE

Dates

It is preferable to include years only, to avoid the margin becoming cluttered. It you started and finished in one year only, put down the year. If it was a vacation job, put down the year and then underneath it put the 'Vacation Work' in brackets. For example: 2007 (Vacation Work). If it is your current job, put 2007-present.

Job title and company details

Use bold type for this, as it will then stand out from the rest of the text.

Main body of text

This is the introductory text. You need to give a brief description of the company, including parameters such as turnover, profitability, number of employees and ownership. Then go on to explain what your role involved. For example, if you were an account manager, what was the value of the accounts you were handling? How many customers did you have? What was your level of responsibility and power? How many staff did you have reporting to you? To whom did you report? What was the management style of the company?

Sample work experience section

Below is an example of a work experience section of the CV (one previous post only), put together in the way outlined in this chapter. Here, the key responsibilities have been set out in a list one below the other for clarity, although you will find that in the sample CVs in Chapter 9 they are combined in one concise paragraph.

1999-present **Senior Accountant, The Borough Council, London**

The Borough Council provides local amenities for council tax payers, residents and visitors, with an annual budget of £17.2 million. Reporting to the Assistant Director of Finance with one direct report. Key responsibilities include:

- Preparing budgets in consultation with senior management.
- Monitoring spending against budgets and providing relevant, accurate and timely information for budget holders.
- Closing accounts and preparing accruals and prepayments.
- Calculating grant claims, liaising with government departments and external auditors.
- Appraising capital projects.
- Preparing and reporting government statistics.

Write the most detailed information on the three most recent companies, but try to keep your CV under three pages. A concise CV will hold the employer's attention better than a waffly four or five-page one.

SIX

Demonstrating your Capabilities

This section is your opportunity to sell yourself and sing your own praises – but softly, of course. Here you will demonstrate to the prospective employer what skills you will bring into the job. The emphasis is on skills, not skill, because like a tree you need strong roots that indicate clearly your many areas of expertise. The task will be made a lot easier if you have the job description or advertisement in front of you. Then, you can customize your capabilities to the particular vacancy.

Capability headings

Read through the advertisement or job description and underline the key capability headings. If you are making a speculative application, read through similar advertisements and make up your own headings based on these. You should have between four or five headings, depending upon the space given to each. For the heading title, the clues are in the advertisement itself: what is it asking that the applicant has done or is able to do? As a general rule, there will always be the Personal section for reflecting your personality and the Technical section. The latter relates to the profession, so it might be headed Finance, Sales, Design, Engineering or Writing, for example. The remaining three headings might cover areas such as:

- Leadership and Management
- Administration

- Communication
- Computing
- Operations and Methods
- Commercial
- Teaching
- Training

You should be aiming for a balanced capabilities section – it is not impressive if you have ten technical capabilities and nothing else to your name.

Once you have chosen your five capability headings, you are ready to write the detailed content for each section. To help you in this process, a list is provided overleaf of words that are frequently used to describe the doing functions. These words are all 'active' ones – words that create a positive impact, which is what you are after. Read the list and highlight the skills that you feel confident about applying in your new job.

Putting your capabilities on paper

Now it is time to write about your skills/capabilities, following the format on page 90. Use each of your highlighted words to start a sentence and then go on to describe how you can perform the required task. Express your ideas clearly and with as much detail as possible, but again, try not to write to impress – it rarely works and often switches off the reader. The examples given, the list of doing words and the sample CVs in Chapter 9 should give you a good idea of what is required.

Activating
Acquiring
Adapting
Adding
Adjusting
Administering
Advising
Analysing
Applying
Appointing
Appraising
Arranging
Assembling
Assigning
Auditing
Awarding
Balancing
Building
Buying
Calculating
Calling
Changing
Charging
Checking
Classifying
Collating
Collecting
Combining
Committing
Communicating
Comparing
Compiling
Completing
Conducting research
Confirming
Consolidating
Constructing
Consulting
Contracting
Contributing
Corresponding
Creating
Deciding
Delegating
Describing
Detecting
Determining
Developing
Devising
Directing
Discussing
Dispatching
Dividing
Drafting
Drawing
Driving
Editing
Encouraging
Endorsing
Enforcing
Enlarging
Ensuring
Entertaining
Establishing
Estimating
Evaluating
Examining
Exchanging
Experimenting
Explaining
Familiarizing
Filing
Forecasting
Formulating
Furnishing
Generating
Granting
Guiding
Hiring
Illustrating
Improving
Informing
Initiating
Inspecting
Instructing
Interpreting
Interviewing
Investigating
Joining
Judging
Justifying
Keeping abreast of
Keeping informed of
Keeping records
Leading
Learning quickly
Lecturing
Listening
Listing
Making decisions
Managing
Measuring
Meeting
Modifying
Monitoring
Motivating
Negotiating
Notifying
Obtaining
Operating equipment
Organizing
Persuading
Planning
Presenting
Preventing
Pricing
Probing
Programming
Promoting
Proof-reading
Proposing
Providing
Questioning
Rating
Reading
Recommending
Reconciling
Recording
Recruiting
Relating
Reporting
Representing
Resolving
Reviewing
Scheduling
Searching
Securing
Selecting
Selling
Serving
Simplifying
Sketching
Solving
Sorting
Standardizing
Stimulating
Studying
Suggesting
Summarizing
Supervising
Supporting others
Surveying
Testing
Training
Transcribing
Translating
Travelling
Typing
Validating
Verifying
Warning
Watching
Working
Working
Writing

Sample Sentences – Create your own

Doing word	How you perform the task, and the outcome
Anticipating	problems and developing plans to address them when they arise.
Persuading and influencing	others without using formal authority and thus building trustworthy business relationships.
Managing and motivating	staff to achieve clear and concise goals.
Interviewing and employing	high-quality people with different cultures, backgrounds and experience, from both inside and outside the organization
Designing and implementing	control procedures to improve the company's cash flow.

Have a go: it is not as difficult as it seems. Although it may be time consuming, it is confidence building to remind yourself of your individual value.

SEVEN

Achievements Count

This chapter is about clarifying what you have done in your job(s) and life. Achievements count. By highlighting them, your CV will have greater impact and become memorable: employers tend to refer to candidates as 'he/she was the one that did such and such'. Achievements demonstrate to the prospective employer that you are an achiever and/or creator and not just another dutiful worker. Remember: duties are not results, they are your obligation to the company.

Achievements need to be SMART: Specific, Measurable, Accurate, Relevant and Timely. First, you must clarify any accomplishments by referring to dates, figures and facts, and/or by supplying any other information which gives the reader a clear indication of your successes.

Most people find having to clarify their achievements a daunting prospect, mainly because they feel that they haven't done anything amazing. Consequently, they either leave out this section completely or gloss over it. However, achievements are a vital part of the CV, for they are your track record and what makes you stand out from the competition.

Everyone has at least one achievement to put down under each job section. Perhaps you suggested something, implemented something, were complimented on something, changed something or improved something. Reflect on what you have done in your job and I am sure you will find you have achieved more than you give yourself credit for.

Putting your achievements on paper

Follow the tips below when writing about your achievements.

- An achievement represents what you have contributed to a job. Achievements don't have to be earth shattering, but if they are, so much the better.
- Include three to five achievements for each job.
- Write short sentences – two or three lines at most.
- Indent the paragraphs so that the achievements are visible.
- Put the achievements in order of importance and acclaim.
- Use simple terms to describe what you did.
- Include quantities, amounts and value to enhance the descriptions.

Listed on page 94 are words that reflect achievements. Identify and circle all those that you believe are the experiences that the employer is seeking.

Now use one of these verbs to start a sentence and then go on to describe your achievements, adding detail and emphasis for clarity. Refer to the job advertisement, if available, as this may give you an indication of the types of things to include, and use the examples below to help you write concisely and effectively. If necessary, refer to the sample CVs in Chapter 9 for ideas and clarity.

Achievement word	How/what/when it was accomplished
Generated	six new clients and an additional 20 per cent in fees in the last financial year.
Contributed	to the achievement of a sales performance 10 per cent above target.
Wrote and implemented	a computer system that improved management reporting.
Commended	for attendance record, personable manner and accuracy.

So have a go at recalling all you have achieved within your roles. You may be quietly surprised to see just how big a contribution you have made.

Verbs of Achievement

Acquired
Administered
Advised
Analysed
Arranged
Assembled
Assisted
Built
Calculated
Collected
Completed
Conducted
Consolidated
Constructed
Controlled
Corresponded
Counselled
Created
Delivered
Designed
Detected
Determined
Developed
Devised
Directed
Discovered
Dispensed
Distributed
Drew up
Edited
Eliminated
Evaluated
Examined
Expanded
Formulated
Generated
Identified
Implemented
Improved
Increased
Installed
Instructed
Interpreted
Interviewed
Invented
Lectured
Logged
Maintained
Managed
Negotiated
Networked
Observed
Obtained
Operated
Organized
Oversaw
Performed
Planned
Prepared
Presented
Processed
Produced
Programmed
Promoted
Protected
Provided
Purchased
Received
Recommended
Recorded
Reduced
Referred
Represented
Researched
Restored
Reviewed
Revised
Rewarded
Selected
Served
Sold
Solved
Studied
Supervised
Supplied
Tested
Trained
Translated
Wrote

EIGHT

CV Style

The style of the CV is important. Primarily, you need to conform to the employer's requirements. In the UK employers prefer a two or three page, full CV to a flashy, one-page effort. Secondly, you need to personalize the CV.

The 'new look' CV

The CV style suggested here and demonstrated in Chapter 9 has proved to be highly successful. It is a 'new look' combination CV written in ordinary, everyday English and incorporating capabilities, achievements and personality sections, and has won approval across the board for its comprehensiveness, conformity and vision. This combination CV will help you to 'sell' yourself – the whole person, rather than just your previous job titles as with the typical chronological-type CV. It is a very 'open' style of CV, unlike the 'functional' CV which contains little else but the straight forward functional headings. This new look CV acts as a useful interviewing document and will provide you, the candidate, with more positive interviews than you may have been uscd to.

Presentation is also important, and this includes the number of pages, paper and fonts used, as well as the way in which the CV itself is laid out.

Length

To reiterate: your CV should be only two or three pages in length. Anything more and you run the risk of it not even being read. Don't worry about leaving something out: you can't possibly include everything you have ever done. Use only the major and relevant facts and you will then keep the employer happy and still achieve your three-page limit. If you have been a bit brief over something you can always elaborate on it at the interview.

Don't cram everything on to these two pages so that the text looks squashed. There must be sufficient white space around it to be kind to the eyes.

Paper and fonts

If you are considering printing your CV, stick to a good-quality white paper. Don't try to be flash by using coloured paper – it doesn't work.

If you can print off every CV individually rather than photocopying an original, you will create a better impression. A photocopied CV is regarded as a bit of a 'shoddy' effort, especially as a bureau will print off CVs for a relatively small charge.

Layout

The sample CVs provided in Chapter 9 demonstrate a successful layout which is clear, easy to read and gives maximum impact to each part of the CV.

NINE

Sample CVs

A number of sample CVs are provided on the following pages. These are real CVs compiled by some of my clients and they demonstrate the types of things to include under certain professions. The names and identities of individuals and companies have all been changed to protect the people concerned.

Read through these CVs and use them to help you to create your own, but remember to modify and alter the examples as necessary because the finished result must ***be your perfect CV***.

A Banking CV

JOB TARGET – BUSINESS DEVELOPMENT MANAGER

Profession *Banking*
Field *Private Banking*
Company *Another bank or building society*
Salary *At least £55,000*
Special requirements *Less than 30 minutes travelling time* *Company pension*
Current employment status *Full-time employment, concerned about being made redundant following company takeover*

PETER HARRIS

PERSONAL DETAILS

Some Street, Ealing, London SW13 3QQ

British, married with one child

Home Telephone: xxxxx xxxxx
Mobile: xxxxx xxxxxx
Email: email@internet.com

CAPABILITIES

Private & Property Lending Banker

- Demonstrating an established track record in business development and relationship management within the SME sector.
- Applying 15 years of comprehensive experience within the lending, insurance premium financing, property finance, deposit taking, treasury and asset management sectors.
- Reading technical publications, journals and articles to keep up-to-date with changes and shifts in the market.

Commercial

- Analysing the company's key performance measures and taking suitable actions to improve them.
- Establishing customer needs and working out how to best deliver the result.
- Developing concepts and opportunities with customers that may not have been previously identified and explored.
- Negotiating contracts with customers and clients including agreeing service levels and terms and conditions to ensure customer satisfaction and economic viability.
- Generating remunerative lending business for a number of City financial institutions using strong interpersonal skills.

Communication

- Communicating ideas clearly on paper, on a one-to-one basis and to small and large audiences.
- Balancing the demands of the operation against the administration.
- Building and maintaining good relationships with staff and service users in person and over the telephone.
- Presenting to all kinds of audiences with confidence and poise to ensure a high retention of knowledge.
- Translating financial data into concise, relevant and user-friendly reports.

Personal

- Learning to adapt to different commercial environments quickly and with ease.
- Regularly seeking opportunities to improve business performance.
- Setting high but achievable standards of performance both personally and for others.

PETER HARRIS

CAREER HISTORY

2004 - Present **Business Development Manager, The Commerce Bank, London**
An independent Commercial Finance Broker which arranges all types of finance for UK owner-managed businesses. Reporting to the Sales & Marketing Director, responsibilities include generating commercial lending enquiries, meeting clients, securing mandates and approaching financial institutions on behalf of clients within the house-building, leisure, property investment, manufacturing and service sectors. Placing deals ranging from £100k to £10m and negotiating optimum financial packages for a range of companies.
Major Achievements:

- Arranged debt and equity finance for clients including an £8.5m commercial investment loan for a property investor.
- Placed commercial lending business with financial institutions.
- Developed a strong network of introducers including accountants, business transfer agents, general insurance brokers, independent financial advisers, property agents and lawyers.

2000 - 2003 **Business Development Manager - Property Lending / Deposit Taking, Global Bank Limited, London**
A specialist property lending bank. Reporting to the Managing Director, responsibilities included generating both deposit and property lending business enquiries, meeting clients, structuring appropriate deals and presenting them for approval by the Credit Committee.
Major Achievements:

- Doubled the sterling deposit base within months from £7m to £14m.
- Secured profitable performing loans worth approximately £8m after introducing numerous quality lending opportunities within the residential development sector.

1994 - 2000 **Manager - Banking and Treasury, LKP, London**

1993 - 1994 **Consultant working in Poland & Russia**

1990 - 1993 **Credit Analyst and Loans Administrator, Trading Bank, London**
1988 - 1989 **Cashier / Foreign Exchange & Securities Clerk, Midland Bank, London**

EDUCATION

Fellow, The Securities& Investment Institute (FSI). **Associate,** The Chartered Institute of Bankers (ACIB).
Member, The Guild of International Bankers. **Member,** The Institute of Directors.

Certificate in Mortgage Advice and Practice (CeMAP), 2003

Three A-Levels, Nine O-Levels, Ashville College, Harrogate, 1987

A Design CV

JOB TARGET – SENIOR GRAPHIC DESIGNER

Profession *Design*
Field *Graphic Design for Print*
Company *Design company with household name/blue chip clients*
Salary *At least £45,000*
Special requirements *Working flexible hours, company car, private health care and company pension*
Current employment status *Fed up in current role - need a new challenge ASAP*

PAUL ADAMS

PERSONAL DETAILS

3 Anywhere Drive, Bristol, BR7 7ZQ

British, Married

Home Telephone: xxxx xxxxx
Mobile: xxxxx xxxxxx
Email: email@internet.com

CAPABILITIES

Design

- Generating and writing creative ideas in a 'down-to-earth' and easy-to-read style.
- Designing logos and advertising layouts to create visual designs for annual reports and other corporate literature.
- Liaising with clients, suppliers and external contractors from the initial design concept through to completion.
- Budgeting to client and company set requirements for budgets as large as £5k.

Leadership and Management

- Recruiting and developing teams of art workers and designers to maximise their output.
- Managing, motivating and training staff to achieve company targets and standards.
- Leading a team by example, monitoring progress and generating ideas.

Administration and Communication

- Communicating regularly with team colleagues, employees and third parties over the phone to keep up-to-date with contracts, company policies and procedures.
- Encouraging good working relationships between all employees and customers alike.
- Communicating by phone to employees to provide effective solutions to any queries.
- Suggesting practical ways to senior management of improving the company's performance.

Personal

- Communicating and presenting design concepts verbally and visually to all levels of personnel within an organization.
- Meeting deadlines, ensuring projects and contracts are completed on target.
- Travelling abroad to solve customer's operational problems.
- Improving personal and technical skills through courses, self-study and dedication.

EDUCATION

Computer Graphics and Advanced Computer Graphics Vocational Courses, Some University, 1998

HND in Technical Graphics, A School of Art, Burton-on-Trent, Staff, 1994

Seven GCSEs A Comprehensive School, Staffs, 1991

PAUL ADAMS

CAREER HISTORY

2002 - Present

Senior Mac Designer, An Advertising Firm, Bristol
A highly successful partnership in the graphic design and advertising industry with £10m annual turnover. Reporting to the Creative Head of the Company, responsibilities include managing the production of a wide range of UK and foreign sales and promotional literature whilst managing a team of five support staff. Also maintain Apple Mac computer equipment and liaise with repro houses and other imaging bureaux.
Major Achievements:

- Safeguarded the company's assets by recommending and implementing new file backup practices.
- Improved design productivity by introducing new software to supplement existing software.
- Introduced and developed the facility to produce in-house digital artwork on high-resolution input and output scanners.
- Improved team effectiveness by prioritising workloads.

1994 - 2002

Designer, A Design Firm, Wells, Somerset
A well established and successful design company used by many well-known national and local clients with £6m turnover. Reporting to the Design and Publishing Manager, responsibilities included costing and developing client briefs whilst liaising with repro houses, printers and multi-media/video sub-contractors. Also oversaw staff training and the evaluation and implementation of new hardware and software products including QuarkXpress, Adobe Photoshop, Adobe Illustrator, Adobe Dimensions, Macromedia Director, Aldus Persuasion and Microsoft PowerPoint.
Major Achievements:

- Ensured better customer service after evaluating and implementing new equipment worth £45k.
- Oversaw the use of all audio-visual media at a major Conference.
- Improved efficiency and working practices by networking the company's Apple Macs and PCs.
- Supervised production of a quarterly journal with an annual £5k budget.

A Finance CV

JOB TARGET – FINANCE DIRECTOR

Profession *Accountancy*
Field *Corporate Finance*
Company *Major FMCG or manufacturing company*
Salary *Min. £55,000*
Special requirements *Within an hour's commuting distance, company car, private health care and company pension*
Current employment status *Within three months*

ANDREW TAYLOR
BSc (Hons) FMCA

PERSONAL DETAILS

A Lovely Drive, Tunbridge Wells, Kent, TU7 3LR

British, Married with two children

Home Telephone: xxxxx xxxxx
Mobile: xxxxx xxxxxx
Email: email@internet.com

CAPABILITIES

Financial

- Comparing actual financial results against budget and analysing variances.
- Ensuring that transactions and financial reports are compliant with International Accounting Standards.
- Measuring and reconciling trading profit and loss on a daily basis and resolving any discrepancies promptly.
- Coordinating with external auditors to ensure effective and timely financial year-end audit procedures.
- Using standard systems including the MS Office Suite (Excel, Word, PowerPoint) ... Reuters 3000 Xtra ... Bloomberg ... Financial CAD ... Integra-T treasury management software ... and SAP R/3.

Strategic Planning

- Establishing an early understanding of the business and its sector and market by getting involved in the 'sharp end', meeting key staff, and reviewing past financials and future budgets.
- Reviewing all areas to obtain an accurate 'top level' view of strengths and weaknesses as well as any crucial issues.
- Interpreting the results against sector and business knowledge to generate a range of actions such as enhancing pay rates to secure better staff or increasing marketing spend to raise the company's profile.
- Screening, valuing and visiting acquisition target companies and reporting recommendations to the board.

Management

- Assigning clear areas of responsibility, delegating and prioritizing appropriately.
- Creating an environment that rewards collaboration, mutual support and achievement of goals.
- Motivating and leading project teams and monitoring progress.
- Reorganising departments and systems to improve efficiency of working practices.
- Chairing meetings, ensuring they run to time, cover the published agenda and achieve results.

Personal

- Displaying control and flexibility in complex or stressful situations.
- Getting to the heart of problems by focusing on critical information and issues.
- Demonstrating initiative and resourcefulness in order to achieve tangible results.

EDUCATION & QUALIFICATIONS

Fellow, Chartered Institute of Management Accountants, 1997
BSc (Hons) (2:1) in Accounting & Finance, Some University, 1993
Three A Levels, A Sixth Form College, Shropshire, 1990

ANDREW TAYLOR
BSc (Hons) FMCA

CAREER HISTORY

2002 - Present **Financial Controller, A Retail Plc, London**
A leading British retailer of consumer durable goods with more than £1.1bn turnover. Reporting to the Financial Director, responsibilities include advising the management of the financial impact of their decisions whilst supervising five direct reports in a 50 employee department. Develop financial and appraisal systems which match profitability and growth requirements and oversee the implementation of new fully integrated SAP R/3 systems. Also influenced the business' strategic direction.
Major Achievements:
- Reduced borrowing from £1m to £500k by implementing a treasury management system.
- Saved approximately £1m after identifying and implementing cost reductions over six months.
- Selected as sole company representative on CBI Fast-Track course for leading young management.
- Improved reporting and control systems, tracking cash position, profitability, investments and liquidity.
- Implemented reporting and job evaluation changes following a divisional management development audit.

1998 **Financial Accountant, The Same plc, London**
Reporting to the Financial Controller, responsibilities included preparing financial accounts for the plc and its subsidiaries for submission to the auditors whilst supervising three direct reports. Provided financial analyses and comparisons against operating budgets and ensured that financial accounts gave a true and fair reflection of the company's performance.
Major Achievements:
- Evaluated future product investments values between £5m and £20m.
- Achieved zero audit points for four consecutive years.
- Led and chaired a cross-functional management team successfully to complete a £1.5m product launch.

1995 - 1998 **Management Accountant, A Music plc, London**
A global leader in the fast-moving and dynamic music industry, with £1.1bn worldwide turnover. Reporting to the Financial Director, responsibilities included managing the financial evaluation and movement of stock and work-in-progress, controlling the purchase ledger and analysing the sales ledger. Helped prepare taxation schedules, consolidated and reported monthly management accounts and developed and implemented new systems as needed.
Major Achievements:
- Ensured that essential information was produced efficiently, on time and to a consistent standard after devising a budgetary control spreadsheet.
- Improved the quality of business decisions through regular presentations of concise and relevant financial information.
- Standardised and improved month-end procedures across departments, including all relevant spending data.

1993 - 1995 **Regional Finance Trainee, A Company Ltd, London**

A first job

JOB TARGET – TRAINEE REPORTER

Profession
Journalism
Field
News Reporting
Company
Local Newspapers/Magazines
Salary
Around £20,000
Special requirements
Good career advancement and prospects
Current employment status
Available immediately

CHRISTINE LLOYD

PERSONAL DETAILS

Some Avenue, Cambridge, CM23 9LD

British, single

Home Telephone: xxxxx xxxxx
Mobile: xxxxx xxxxxx
Email: email@internet.com

CAPABILITIES

Writing

- Visualising and producing imaginative and interesting work with punchy headlines.
- Understanding and following specifications and producing quality work.
- Writing, editing and proof reading to produce a high standard of work.

Research & Analysis

- Generating and contributing creative ideas after researching concepts from a wide variety of sources.
- Collating diverse material to generate outlines leading to first draft treatments and presentations/storyboards.
- Keeping abreast of technology and how best to implement it for a particular job.

Leadership

- Organising logistics that effectively use team members and resources whilst optimising the underlying workflows and technical requirements.
- Coordinating tasks and managing multiple demands whilst responding quickly to changing circumstances.
- Recommending courses of action which are clear and realistic to ensure positive action from all parties.
- Training new staff on all aspects of the business.

Communication

- Communicating regularly with team colleagues, employees and third parties over the phone to keep up-to-date with contracts, company policies and procedures.
- Suggesting practical ways to senior management of improving the company's performance.
- Collaborating well with people at all levels whilst constantly seeking new contributors and constructive partnerships and developing creative team members.

Personal

- Working long hours to achieve personal and company objectives.
- Setting clear goals and focusing on quality to deliver desired outcomes.
- Showing resourcefulness in responding to changing demands and opportunities.
- Displaying initiative and independence, and can work on own or as part of a team, referring to others when necessary.
- Projecting poise and confidence and acting appropriately in business situations.

CHRISTINE LLOYD

EDUCATION

Secretarial Course: Teeline Shorthand 80 wpm ... Typing RSA Level III ... Basic Word Processing, A College, Cambridge, 2006

Three 'A' Levels – English Language (B), Art and Design (B), Media Studies (C), The Sixth Form College, Cambridge, 2004

Eight GCSEs including Maths, English and Science, Some School for Girls, Cambridge, 2002

WORK EXPERIENCE

2006 - Present — **Voluntary Work, Local Radio, Cambridge**
Working as a Saturday Helper. Responsibilities include attending outside broadcasts and helping with the equipment. Also make photocopies, manage mail, answer the telephone and deal with queries and complaints as needed.

Other Media Achievements:

- Wrote an article for a regional newspaper on the problems between New Age travellers, police and the County Council after conducting interviews with all parties and presenting a balanced account of the situation.
- Sold 2,000 copies and raised £3,000 for charity over the 18-month period after researching popular material, generating local business support and setting up a team of six people to produce and edit a quarterly College Newspaper.
- Wrote an article on 'The Beauty of the Cambridgeshire Countryside' which was published on the front page of the local newspaper.
- Won a £1,000 prize in a creative writing competition.

2004 — **Waitress, The Tea Shop, Cambridge**
Responsibilities included working as part of a team, taking orders, serving customers, collecting monies, clearing tables and training new recruits.

2003 - 2004 (Vacation Work) — **Groom, Local Stables, Cambridge**
Responsibilities included training and preparing yearlings for sale, riding racehorses and grooming top horses for international competition. Also supervised the yard and farm as required.

A Nursing CV

JOB TARGET – STAFF NURSE (E GRADE)

Profession *Health Care*
Field *Nursing*
Company *Local NHS or Private Hospital*
Salary *Around £27,000*
Special requirements *Safe area when leaving night shift*
Current employment status *Ready for next move - ASAP*

GRACE BROWN

PERSONAL DETAILS

A Road, Acton Town, London, W3 9QW

British, Single

Telephone: xxxxx xxxxxx
Mobile: xxxxx xxxxxx
Email: email@internet.com

CAPABILITIES

Clinical

- Prioritising, organising and maintaining high standards of care for patients by following nursing process and nursing models such as ROPER.
- Evaluating and presenting patient care effectively to other members of staff via written reports, verbal discussions and formal handovers.
- Liaising and working as part of a MDT team to achieve high standards of individual patient care.
- Listening and talking to patients about their diagnosis, altered body image, psychological problems and future care.

Management

- Following instructions and making decisions when administering the care needs.
- Assisting in the general management of the ward, taking charge when required.
- Ensuring the safe custody and administration of drugs according to the hospital's procedure and policy.
- Maintaining a safe clinical environment for patients and staff.
- Assisting the economical ordering of supplies to ensure efficiency and timeliness.

Professional

- Being accountable for nursing care and actions by complying with the nursing UKCC code of practice.
- Keeping up to date with nursing trends and developments.
- Carrying out instructions as required.

Teaching

- Writing precise, detailed care plans on the patient's actual and potential problems or needs.
- Teaching and advising patients of the nursing knowledge needed to maintain their own health care and learning to recognize potential problems.
- Giving presentations to groups of students and staff.

Personal

- Displaying a cheerful and tactful disposition even in challenging situations.
- Embracing new and challenging projects with a 'can do' attitude.
- Focusing on issues by concentrating on critical information, tasks and issues at the heart of the team.

GRACE BROWN

CAREER HISTORY

2002 - Present **Staff Nurse (Bowel Ward), A Hospital, London**
A specialist bowel centre dealing with national cases of cancer and bowel disease. Responsibilities include admitting patients, evaluating patient care, prioritising work, and assisting in the general management of the ward.
Major Achievements:
- Received excellent appraisals and commended for patient bedside manner and professional approach in emergency cases.
- Built excellent working relationships with members of staff and gained valuable managerial experience.
- Developed listening and counselling skills while dealing with patient diagnoses, psychological problems and future care.
- Attended numerous study days to keep up to date with ongoing medical developments.

2001 - 2004 **Student Nurse, A Good School of Nursing and Midwifery, London**
Responsibilities included gaining specialist experience while training in oncology, urology and renal nursing.
Major Achievements:
- Corresponded, arranged and completed a four-week elective oncology placement at Clatterbridge Hospital in the Wirral.
- Researched and wrote a variety of course projects encompassing cot death, a psychiatric case study of a chosen patient and patient teaching concerning diet.
- Attended resuscitation and fire lectures and a two-day study course Continuing Assessment on Project 2000.

2000 - 2001 **Independent Travel in the United States, Australia and New Zealand**
Gained international and cultural experience.

1997 - 1999 **Voluntary Work for the St John Ambulance**
Attended weekly local events around Guildford to provide necessary medical services and gain basic first aid training experience.

EDUCATION

RGN, Some College of Nursing and Diploma of Nursing, City University, 2004

Three A-Levels ... **Five GCSEs**, A Good School, Guildford, Surrey 2000

A One-Job CV

JOB TARGET – ADMINSTRATION

Profession *Administration*
Field *Office Admin and Systems*
Company *Large stable company with job security*
Salary *At least £30,000*
Special requirements *More than 24 days holiday, fairly standard hours with overtime*
Current employment status *Recently made redundant* *Available immediately*

DAVID BROWN

PERSONAL DETAILS

Some Road,
York, Y01 7RR
British, single

Home Telephone: xxxxx xxxxxx
Mobile: xxxxx xxxxxx
Email: email@internet.com

CAPABILITIES

Administration/Clerical

- Writing business letters, memos and emails stating clearly the facts and situation.
- Keeping detailed and accurate records of transactions.
- Monitoring, analysing and evaluating projects to ensure they are completed on time.

Communication

- Promoting and selling the company's services in a professional manner.
- Building good relationships with customers and colleagues in person or over the telephone.
- Listening to customers and advising them on matters raised.
- Communicating ideas clearly on paper, and also to small groups.
- Contributing ideas to a team to ensure that goals are achieved and deadlines met.

Management

- Leading a team by example, monitoring progress and generating ideas.
- Managing, motivating and supporting staff to build a successful team.
- Listening to other people's ideas and developing them further.
- Making decisions quickly and decisively while maintaining high standards of accuracy.
- Organizing and planning in order to maximize efficiency and performance.
- Meeting deadlines by planning and prioritizing objectives and tasks.

Computing

- Operating the latest computer equipment, systems and software (Bank System-Windows).
- Learning and updating skills as new systems are introduced.

Personal

- Learning quickly to adapt to new working environments and concepts.
- Making decisions confidently to ensure the best end-result to the customer.
- Demonstrating a positive and professional business manner.

DAVID BROWN

CAREER HISTORY

1984 - Present **Personal Banking Officer, A Well Known Bank plc**
One of the four main UK banks employing over 100,000 people.

2003 - Present **Merge Team Leader, A Well Known Bank plc, York**
Reporting to the Operations Manager, supervise a team of seven staff responsible for achieving stated goals following the amalgamation of two bank branches.

Major Achievements:

- Completed the amalgamation within the allocated two-year period.
- Trained new and junior staff to the required proficiency level.

1996 – 2003 **Foreign Clerk, A Well Known Bank plc, Harrogate**
Reporting to the Head of Department, responsibilities included dealing with foreign cheques, currency accounts, forward exchange contracts and travel insurance/money. Completing and processing applications to send money abroad, liaising with international department regarding payment of import/export documents.

Major Achievements:

- Organized security lectures which have improved overall branch security.
- Formulated new working patterns to maximize customer service.
- Generated additional sales in bank travel products when working as foreign/travel services advisor.

1989 - 1996 **Securities Clerk, A Well Known Bank plc, Harrogate**
Reporting to the Securities Manager, responsibilities included dealing with solicitors/executors following the death of a customer and providing information before funds may be of boxes, parcels and certificates lodged for safe keeping on the of boxes, parcels and certificates lodged for safekeeping on the bank's premises.

1984 - 1989 **Personal Banking/Lending, A Well Known Bank plc, Harrogate:** interviewing customers regarding credit control; keeping record of overdrafts; analysing balance sheets.

EDUCATION

Six GCSEs, Sheridon Comprehensive, York, 1984

In-house courses attended include:
Mortgage Enquiry Officer ... Lending for the Personal Banker ... Supervisory Management ... and the Assistant Manager

---

A Sales CV

JOB TARGET – NATIONAL SALES ACCOUNT MANAGER

Profession *Sales*
Field *Account Management*
Company *Large company with opportunities and advancement*
Salary *At least £45,000*
Special requirements *Working flexible hours, company car, private health care and company pension*
Current employment status *Full-time employment, no hurry to move and looking for something over the next year*

MICHAEL FLETCHER
BA (Hons)

PERSONAL DETAILS

Some Drive, Aylesbury,
Buckinghamshire, HW6 2LA
British, Single

Home Telephone: xxxxx xxxxx
Mobile: xxxxx xxxxxx
Email: email@internet.com

CAPABILITIES

Media Sales

- Co-ordinating the daily distribution of national newspapers to wholesale houses.
- Achieving agreed sales, returns and availability targets within national and area budgets.
- Demonstrating workable sales initiatives through presentations and reports.
- Forecasting and calculating trade sales figures during national promotions.
- Analysing and reporting on the opposition's trade promotions and activities.
- Gathering and calculating sales order rates and costs to achieve company targets.

Negotiation

- Negotiating commercial contracts, including terms of payment and guaranteed service levels.
- Organising and running localised promotional events to raise public awareness of the company's products.
- Negotiating with customers to ensure the implementation of national sales promotions.

Management

- Interviewing, recruiting and building quality sales teams to perform different tasks.
- Training, supervising and monitoring canvassing teams to improve and sustain order rates.
- Creating an environment that rewards collaboration, mutual support and achievement of goals.

Personal

- Identifying the "big picture" quickly and clearly and establishing clear project focus.
- Contributing to the company product reviews and recommending the most effective ways of staying ahead of the competition.
- Adapting to different working environments and travelling with ease and confidence.

EDUCATION

BA (Hons) (2:2) in Geography, Hull University, 1992

Three A Levels, Kettering Sixth Form College, Northamptonshire, 1990
Eight GCSEs, St George's School, Kettering, Northamptonshire, 1988

MICHAEL FLETCHER
BA (Hons)

CAREER HISTORY

2000 - Present **Area Sales Manager, National Newspaper plc, Birmingham**
A leading publisher of newspapers and magazines with £2.5bn turnover. Reporting to the Area Sales Controller, responsibilities include identifying and selling business and product benefits to establish a client base. Supervise ten direct reports covering the Midlands region to identify and develop new customers whilst making informed judgements about business potential with individual accounts.
Major Achievements:
- Exceeded weekly order rate targets by over 20% after training and supervising sales personnel individually and as part of a group.
- Achieved the required 80% availability of the newspaper while minimising returns after revising the distribution schedule.
- Supervised the Midlands Region sales team in a week that featured 'The Summer Floods' story.

1994 - 2000 **Sales Representative, National Newspaper plc, Birmingham**
Reporting to the Area Sales Manager, responsibilities included achieving sales targets in 350 of the 1,800 Midlands region retailers by building strong customer relationships with retailers and keeping up to date with the product portfolio.
Major Achievements:
- Promoted a good image of the company by visiting clients regularly and taking an active interest in their business rather than just servicing their accounts.
- Improved internal communication and decision making by making promotional presentations to the senior management team.
- Developed localised promotions to support national promotions window displays in retail outlets.

1993 - 1994 **Merchandising Manager, A Food Company Ltd, London**
A leading specialist in ready-to-eat fish products. Reporting to the Sales Support Manager, responsibilities included improving the major retailers' in-store display of company products.
Major Achievements:
- Improved sales 20% after developing an innovative on-pack gifting promotion.
- Increased shelf space in a major retail outlet by 50% after securing a long-term display deal.

A Secretarial CV

JOB TARGET – PERSONAL ASSISTANT

Profession *Secretary*
Field *Director's PA*
Company *Local company with ideally strong Green principles*
Salary *Around £28,000*
Special requirements *Working flexible hours for a company that understands family needs* *Good social life*
Current employment status *Full-time employment wishing to make more of a personal contribution to society*

DIANE MORRIS

PERSONAL DETAILS

A Cottage, Lyndhurst, Hampshire, LY3 7UT

British, Married with one child

Home Telephone: xxxxx xxxx
Mobile: xxxxx xxxxxx
Email: email@internet.com

CAPABILITIES

Secretarial

- Booking meeting rooms, managing diaries and making travel arrangements along with preparing rotas for staff.
- Typing letters for correspondence with outside agencies and internal departments.
- Corresponding through customer visits, telephone, emails and letters.
- Chasing external bodies for information required within tight deadlines.
- Using MS Office especially Excel, Word and Outlook for reports and general correspondence.

Leadership

- Assigning clear areas of responsibility to small teams and creating the opportunity for feedback, advice and support.
- Presenting to all kinds of audiences with confidence and poise to ensure a high retention of knowledge.
- Helping others to solve problems to the benefit of the individual and the company as a whole.
- Motivating staff to achieve and maintain high standards of work.
- Understanding and listening to people to build and develop supportive and successful teams.

Administrative

- Balancing the demands of the operation against the administration by always working towards deadlines and also working overtime as required.
- Assessing and diagnosing administration and computer problems and evaluating the most cost-effective strategy.
- Developing, implementing and maintaining Celcat and Kenitex booking systems.
- Attending weekly meetings and taking minutes.
- Learning and operating new computer systems and packages including MS Excel, Access and Word.

Personal

- Quickly adapting to new working environments, concepts and systems.
- Addressing complaints and concerns in a calm, authoritative manner.
- Motivating staff through own personal commitment, an ethic of hard work and a "can always do better" attitude.

DIANE MORRIS

CAREER HISTORY

2000 - Present **Personal Assistant, A Photo Company, Southampton**
A specialist in the provision of photographic images for media organisations. Reporting to the Marketing Director, responsibilities include carrying out all secretarial functions and organising and taking minutes at include all secretarial functions. Also take minutes at monthly departmental meetings.
Major Achievements:
- Completed in-house training courses on all aspects of MS Office.
- Supervised and trained the Archiving Assistant and Departmental Secretary.
- Liaised with vending company to ensure adequate supplies.

1997 – 2000 **Secretary, Altoona, A Medical Company, Hampshire**
A manufacturer and distributor of high-tech medical products. Reporting to the Sales and Marketing Manager, responsibilities included carrying out general secretarial and support duties.
Major Achievements:
- Organised annual sales conferences for about 150 delegates, including hotel and travel arrangements.
- Liaised with printers for sales brochures and literature.
- Self-taught the package WordPerfect on new PC system.

1994 – 1997 **Career break to raise family**

1989 – 1994 **Departmental Secretary, A Retail Company, Southampton**
A retailer and distributor of building supplies. Reporting to the Commercial Manager, responsibilities included providing secretarial support for the busy sales department.
Major Achievement:
- Organised and created a logical and efficient filing system.

1985 - 1989 **Clerical Assistant, A Solicitors Firm, Lyndhurst, Hampshire**
A local solicitor's practice. Responsibilities included answering the telephone, typing, greeting clients and general filing.
Major Achievement:
- Commended for attendance record, personable manner and accuracy.

EDUCATION & QUALIFICATIONS

Pitman's Shorthand 100 words per minute ... **RSA Typing** Stage III (Distinction)
- A Secretarial College, Hampshire, 1987

Four O levels, A Secondary School, 1985

A Graduate's CV

JOB TARGET – TEXTILE DESIGNER

Profession *Design*
Field *Textile Design*
Company *Plenty of opportunities for advancement with good in-house training resources*
Salary *At least £23,000*
Special requirements *None*
Current employment status *Recently graduated* *Available immediately*

ROBERT YOUNG
BA (Hons)

PERSONAL DETAILS

A Road, Welwyn Garden City, Herts, AL2 5TU

Home Telephone: xxxxx xxxxx
Mobile: xxxxx xxxxxx

British, Single

Email: email@internet.com

CAPABILITIES

Textiles & Design

- Recognising and adapting traditional textile designs into contemporary art forms.
- Visualising and drawing the 'designs' of the future and predicting new fabrics and materials.
- Producing fabric designs and drawings to set briefs and customer requirements.
- Creating unusual designs based upon inspiration from historical textiles.
- Contributing flexible design ideas to teams or consultancies and challenging designs of the past.

Research & Analysis

- Conducting research on major companies to establish market trends.
- Studying textiles to establish trends and popularity.
- Identifying key issues and opportunities by interviewing key personnel using a proven set of checklists.
- Corresponding with key accounts over escalated issues and ensuring an accurate understanding of requirements.

Computing

- Operating the latest computer equipment, with a good working knowledge of Apple Mac and Photoshop.
- Learning and operating PC software packages, including word processors and spreadsheets.
- Applying an in-depth knowledge of MS Office to office functions including designing spreadsheets in Excel using macros.

Leadership

- Managing, organising and leading small teams to achieve the best results.
- Presenting ideas and proposals assertively and persuasively.
- Putting others at ease, listening actively and encouraging open discussion.
- Meeting deadlines and handling pressure in a fast-moving environment.

Personal

- Socialising, meeting new people and establishing working relationships with confidence.
- Travelling and working in foreign countries with ease and confidence.
- Learning from experience and demonstrating commitment to continuous learning and growth.

ROBERT YOUNG
BA (Hons)

EDUCATION

BA (Hons) (2:2) in Printed Textiles, A Big University, 2007
Working with paint, other media and computers to develop exceptional drawing, colour and design skills. Also studied fashion, interior and home furnishings to build upon drawing skills, pattern repeats, colour, design thinking, textile technology and professional practices.
Major Achievements:

- Designed and supplied Exeter Training Club with designs for T-shirts and track suits.
- Researched the information necessary to complete a 10,000-word dissertation on the UK training shoes market, including interviewing managers of major sports equipment manufacturers.
- Helped organise a college stand at the London Textiles Exhibition in July 1995 and answered queries whilst manning it during the day.

Three A-Levels ... **Ten GCSEs**, A School, Welwyn Garden City, Herts, 2004

WORK EXPERIENCE

2005 - 2007
(Vacation Work)

Sales Assistant, An Interior Designer, Welwyn
The sole UK importer of French Renaissance textiles. Responsibilities included travelling to France with the proprietor to locate and purchase stock. Also assisted with the general management of the shop whilst helping customers choose materials to suit their home.
Major Achievements:

- Gained experience in the history of European textiles and wrote a 10,000-word special project on this subject.

2004 - 2005
(Vacation Work)

Sales Assistant, Most Profitable UK Retailer, Bath
Responsibilities included packing shelves, operating the tills, carry-to-car service and customer service.
Major Achievements:

- Facilitated a prosecution by reporting swiftly to management about a shoplifter,
- Commended for professional manner in dealing with a customer's complaint.

An Engineering CV

JOB TARGET – MANUFACTURING ENGINEERING MANAGER

Profession
Engineering
Field
Production and Manufacturing
Company
Large company in expanding market
Salary
More than £35,000 plus overtime
Special requirements
Ideally days and double shifts *With consider triple shifts as long as within close commuting distance*
Current employment status
Worried about redundancy - need to move quickly

RAJA SINGH

PERSONAL DETAILS

A Road, Old Town, Swindon, SN8 4PX

British, Married with two children

Home Telephone: xxxxx xxxxx
Mobile: xxxxx xxxxxx
Email: email@internet.com

CAPABILITIES

Production Engineering

- Reading and analysing product reliability and field data, taking necessary corrective action decisions.
- Communicating to others what Total Quality Management (TQM) is and what it means to employees, the company and to customers.
- Designing logical procedures to achieve BS5750/IS09002.
- Investigating and diagnosing the source of manufacturing faults and product failures in implementing a development programme.
- Presenting the case for implementing TQM, MRP 2, JIT, FMS and manufacturing cells so that the company stays at the leading edge of manufacturing technology.

Management

- Interviewing, selecting and building a dynamic and effective team of engineers.
- Leading and monitoring a team of design, development, manufacturing and quality engineers to turn specifications into finished products.
- Checking that projects specifications satisfy customer requirements.
- Operating and teaching others to use mainframe and personal computers.

Commercial

- Negotiating sales contracts, highlighting the technical benefits to the customer.
- Studying competitor's projects and developing strategies to gain superiority.
- Creating a plan for the introduction of a new product by the most cost-effective route.
- Visualising how a product or process will work and sketching an idea which a designer can turn into a drawing.
- Evaluating development programmes and field trial results, assessing the risk of full scale production.
- Planning the best way of bringing a new product to the market.

Personal

- Challenging working practices and systems and motivating fellow professionals to deliver productivity improvements.
- Listening to others' concerns, evaluating the risks to the company and taking engineering decisions.

EDUCATION

Chartered Member, Institution of Electrical Engineers, 1989

Diploma in Production Engineering, A Technology, London, 1985
HND in Mechanical Engineering, The Same College of Technology, London, 1984
Two A-Levels ... Seven O Levels, A College, London, 1981

RAJA SINGH

CAREER HISTORY

1985 - Present **A Mining Equipment Firm, Swindon, Wilts**
A division of Mining International and an International supplier of coal mining machinery with £65m current sales.

2000 - Present **Engineering Manager**
Responsibilities include overseeing product design and development, shop production engineering, and shop quality whilst managing a team of 12 engineers. Solve problems, produce technical quotations, and analyse and correct complaints;
Major Achievements:
- Helped gain world records for coal output by engineering the key products involved.
- Saved 12% after designing a cost-reduced range of valves.
- Secured BS5750 Part I after providing training for all staff.
- Improved customer service with a comprehensive TQM programme.

1995 – 1997 **Production Manager**
Responsibilities include meet production targets whilst maintaining good industrial relations. Also oversaw cost control, output performance, output quality and staffing.
Major Achievements:
- Maximised the benefits of JIT, FMS and cellular manufacture by implementing improved production methods.
- Designed programmes to ensure the new valves were produced on time, to required quality and cost.
- Wrote a case study, 'Implementation of Computer-aided Manufacture' for the Open University which was made into a television programme.

1995 - 1997 **Chief Manufacturing Engineer**
Responsibilities included managing the production engineering requirements of the assembly and machine shops, including a flexible manufacturing system (FMS).
Major Achievement:
- Translated customer specifications into designs and finished products on time and to budget

1992 - 1995 **Manufacturing Systems Manager**
Introduced Computer-aided process planning, NC Part Programming and Computer-aided Jig and Tool Design.

1985 - 1992 **Value Analysis Engineering roles**
Responsible for organising the department and product cost reduction.

Changing Profession

JOB TARGET – OUTDOOR/INDOOR FITNESS INSTRUCTOR

Profession *Health Advice*
Field *Fitness and Sports Coaching*
Company *Outdoor Pursuit Company working with Adults or Children*
Salary *£23,000*
Special requirements *Boarding facilities and an opportunity to travel in UK and Abroad*
Current employment status *Just left Services available immediately*

SIMON JONES

PERSONAL DETAILS

A Nice Road, Crossland Moor,
Huddersfield, HD2 6DU
British, Single

Home Telephone: xxxxx xxxxx
Mobile: xxxxx xxxxxx
Email: email@internet.com

CAPABILITIES

Sporting

- Training hard but sensibly whilst learning new sporting skills easily and quickly.
- Working productively as a team member to contribute own skills and views.
- Designing weight-lifting programmes for people with different abilities.
- Running marathons in the UK and Germany and also cycling for competition and pleasure.

Coaching & Leadership

- Listening to people's sporting problems, giving advice and providing the necessary support.
- Teaching and training young people the basics of football ... leading and teaching aerobic classes whilst demonstrating new movements ... leading rock climbs in hard and severe conditions ... instructing canoeing up to BCU one star standard to under 16s ... and coaching basketball to achieve good league results.
- Promoting a better understanding of subjects by adapting standardised training materials to suit individuals and group needs.
- Setting high but achievable standards of performance both personally and for others.
- Meeting deadlines by planning and prioritising objectives and tasks.

Communication

- Communicating ideas clearly on paper, on a one-to-one basis and to small and large audiences.
- Writing reports for local newspapers on sporting events.
- Presenting to all kinds of audiences with confidence and poise to ensure a high retention of knowledge.
- Building and maintaining good relationships with staff and service users in person and over the telephone.
- Reading and writing basic German.

Personal

- Planning own day, week and month to set targets and goals and also to "clear own desk" every day as an ambitious, determined and eager individual.
- Listening sympathetically to team member concerns and suggestions.
- Demonstrating enthusiasm, vision, diplomacy and flexibility to motivate employees and partners and see through business changes.

SIMON JONES

CAREER HISTORY

2005 - Present **Plant Engineer, A Local Leisure Centre, Huddersfield**
Work at the centre while self-financing evening courses in Fitness Training. Duties include maintaining the equipment and ensuring facilities are fully operational.
Major Achievements:
- Achieved good results in all Fitness Training courses and commended for thoroughness and accuracy in maintaining the equipment.
- Ran the 80-mile South Downs Way, coming 53rd in 15 hours and 12 minutes and raising £400 for charity.
- Completed the London marathon in 2½ hours and reduced personal best time by 17 minutes.
- Trained a football team of under elevens who improved throughout the season.
- Studied the sport of basketball and achieved a Basketball Leader's Award.
- Performed many classic rock climbs up to a hard standard.

1999 – 2005 **Aircraft Engineering Technician Propulsion, Royal Air Force, Kinloss**
Duties included supervising the aircraft servicing teams to maintain an intensive flying programme. Installed aircraft components in extreme heat and freezing temperatures and helped rectify aircraft to keep them flying in war conditions.
Major Achievements:
- Received invitations to work at RAF Queen's Flight on two occasions.
- Operated many types of aircraft ground equipment whilst overcoming language barriers.
- Trained junior and senior ranks to refuel aircraft prior to short notice detachments abroad.
- Logged 10½ hours' flying time towards a private pilot's licence.
- Passed key air, law and meteorology examinations.

EDUCATION

British Amateur Weight Lifting Association Course (BAWLA), 2005
RSA Diploma in Exercise to Music ... Aerobic Instructor, 1995

Basketball Leader's Award, English Basketball Association, Nov 1995

Six GCSEs, King's School, Torquay, Devon, 1999

TEN

The Covering Letter

A covering letter is an absolute necessity. Without it, the application is naked and incomplete. A CV is not a stand-alone document; it needs a covering letter to confirm and draw out the relevant detail of the CV.

The purpose of the covering letter is to:

- Inform the employer that you are applying for the job.
- Advise that your CV is attached.
- Sell your strengths.
- Supply any additional information requested in the advertisement.
- Cover any concerns that the employer might have about you.

If you send in a CV without a covering letter, you run the risk of your application literally ending up in the bin. Employers may conclude that you are unreliable because (a) you can't complete a task, (b) you can't present yourself properly (so how could you then represent the company?) or (c) you can't write letters.

Of course, for most job hunters it is not that they can't write, but that they find writing a covering letter difficult. This is often because it is normally the last task in the whole application process and by then they have lost enthusiasm. All that matters to them at this stage is to complete the task and get the application in the post before the due date.

Writing a covering letter is difficult. It is actually harder to write than your CV, because you start with a completely clean slate and this can be a bit daunting. At least when you write your

CV you have your background to draw upon, which is a definite pool of information.

This chapter will help you to choose the right style and format for your letter. A good letter has every chance of being read, and most business people will be courteous enough to talk to you on the phone, even if only briefly, if you follow up your leads with a telephone call.

Things to avoid

Most covering letters fail because they don't empower the employer. In other words, they don't add anything more to the application – and sometimes they even destroy the message of the CV itself. This may be because the letter is:

☒ **A weak letter**, which states only that the CV is enclosed, rather than reconfirming your areas of expertise. This type of letter gives the power back to the employer: the power to say 'yes' or 'no' to your application. Unfortunately, most covering letters fall into the 'weak' category.

☒ **An arrogant letter**, which will put off employers. Perhaps it implies or even states why the employer should take on the applicant, or explains how the company should run its business. Try to avoid this approach, as it normally makes the employer aggressive towards you.

☒ **A humorous letter**, which will normally misfire. The joke will almost certainly be on you, and your letter may be passed around the company as a source of amusement. Save your sense of humour for the times when you are face to face with the recipient. You can then judge the response and modify your approach accordingly.

☒ **A creative letter**, which has its place only in the PR, advertising and marketing fields. Here almost anything goes and a letter of this kind will be appreciated, rather than going over the top of the employer's head. However, if you want to be creative and this is not your line of work you can still allow yourself to be different, but more subtly, by choosing a different ending to 'Yours sincerely' or 'Yours faithfully'. You can make up your own, but you could try 'With confidence', 'Regards', 'With great interest', 'Very truly yours', 'Your friend', 'Best regards', 'With warm thanks', and so on.

Types of covering letters

Covering letters fall into certain categories, each one having a different tone, approach and message. Choose the appropriate category and model your letter on the advice and examples provided. The tip is not to copy but to adapt letters you like, because the letter has to be you. It should sound and read like you, because you will have to answer questions about it at an interview or follow it up with a telephone call.

There is no set way of writing a covering letter. The key is to include the important points and to make it yours.

THE COVERING LETTER IN RESPONSE TO AN ADVERTISEMENT

This is perhaps the easiest letter of all to write. The advertisement will give you an indication of the type and amount of information that is required; this letter also has a standard format.

1. **Address the letter to a named person.**
   Personal letters will often be read in preference to standard ones. If the advertisement doesn't give the name, ring up the company and ask for it.

2. **Explain what has made you write.**
   You know why, but the company doesn't. Try to keep your explanation simple, brief and effective:
   'I am replying to your advertisement in the (name the newspaper/journal/magazine) on the (give date).'
   'I understand from a mutual friend (name the person if you have their permission) that a vacancy has been advertised (on the noticeboards, or state where).'
   'I have been referred to you by (name the person), who mentioned that your company is looking to recruit additional (state type of staff).'

3. **Sound enthusiastic about the position.**
   An employer wants to see that you are excited about the job, so include this in your letter. Try to be warm and friendly. You can always tone down what you have written once it is on paper:
   'I am most interested in the possibilities which your position offers.'
   'The challenge offered by your post is one that I would welcome'.

4. **Explain your origin and expertise**.
   You are only of interest to a potential employer if your experience will be of value to him/her. It is harsh, but the work world operates only on value, not need, so avoid the mistake of telling the employer what you are looking for from him/her. To demonstrate your value, you will need to list your key areas of expertise:
   'I am (state number) years of age and have been employed in responsible positions for (list the companies).
   'I have immense experience of (list areas of experience).'

5. **Highlight, don't hide, any disadvantages.**
   This may not apply to you, but if it does don't try to cover up your disadvantages. Admit any shortcomings and then they

will no longer be regarded as such. Rather, it will be seen as a positive sign that you are aware of and are working on them: 'Although I have no practical experience of (state area of expertise required), I do have experience of (state your areas of expertise), and therefore I know I will learn very quickly.'

Sample letter

[*Date*]

Mr G Smith

[*The Address*]

Dear Mr Smith [*Naming the person*]

I am replying to your recent advertisement in the *Financial Times* 29 April 200X and enclose my comprehensive CV [*Explaining what has made you write*]

I am most interested in the possibilities which your position offers. [*Expressing enthusiasm*] Being a qualified accountant, I have immense financial experience and I work at present for a prestigious and profitable company called …

My key areas of expertise are:

- preparing and analysing financial information
- compiling and appraising capital schemes
- managing accounting activities
- motivating and supervising staff
- Operating and using PC equipment and software systems, including ….. [*Explaining your origin and expertise*]

The challenge offered by your post is one I would welcome. [*Reconfirming your enthusiasm for the job*]

I look forward to discussing the job in greater detail at an interview. [*The final sell*]

With great interest [*A different ending*]

[*Your Name*]

COLD/SPECULATIVE COVERING LETTER

Your job target or the job market may mean that you have to introduce yourself to companies in the form of a speculative letter. If you write a good business like letter and fulfil a need, some companies will call you in for a chat/interview, and most will give you feedback on your style and approach over the telephone - such feedback may be vital to your future success.

It is advisable to try several different approaches and if you find that one particular letter creates a good response stick to it, because you know it works!

1. **Be selective in your approach.**

   It is important to mail a small sample of letters first, otherwise it will cost you a small fortune for little or no response, which is very demoralizing. Before you mail your letter, check the standard of writing and design by getting a second opinion. Then send out a few letters: if you get the kind of response from companies that you are looking for, send out this letter on a large scale.

2. **The opening is vital.**

   You don't want your letter to end up in the bin, so try not to tell the reader what his/her company needs or wants. You need to arouse his/her interest by taking about either the company or yourself.

   Talk about the company and by all means compliment them, but it must be genuine:

   'I read your article in (name the newspaper) and I was interested to read that you do ...

   'The company is recognized as a proven expert in the (state field) market. I have always been (fascinated with/interested in the product/image of the company).'

Introduce yourself, but not by saying you can help the company because you don't know that you can or even that you want to:

'In light of your phenomenal growth in 2006, there is a strong probability of growth and expansion for 2007 and beyond. If so, perhaps my enclosed CV will be of interest to you (your let-out clause). My background encompasses all aspects of (state field)...

'My experience and accomplishments in (state number) years of manufacturing should be of interest to you if you need a (state profession) to help guide your organization (your let out clause).'

3. **Explain what role you are looking for.**

   Sell yourself in terms of your expertise first and give an indication of the role you are seeking. Try not to be specific:

   'My key areas of expertise are (refer to the example of the letter in response to an advertisement).

   'I am interested in finding a challenging (state field) position using my key areas of expertise, which would offer an opportunity for career advancement. I am a global-thinking person who believes in serving the marketplace. I would be very valuable to the right organization.'

4. **End the letter properly.**

   Unless you state what action you want, nothing will happen. Tell the employer what action you will take: perhaps you will ring to arrange an appointment to discuss this letter further, or you will call in on them. Then do what you say, because it will not reflect at all well on you if you don't.

5. Asking for referrals

If you are told 'no' and to 'go away', don't. Instead, be brave, ring up and ask for comments on your CV and approach. Don't forget to ask for referrals – names of companies that might need someone with your capabilities. It can do you no harm and may be just the kind of advice you need.

Sample letter

[*Date*]

Mr G Smith

[*The Address*]

Dear Mr Smith [*Naming the person*]

On Tuesday [*give date*] I read your article in [*name the newspaper*]. You may have guessed that your article made quite an impression on me. Not only were your suggestions helpful, but your writing revealed admirable qualities about your company. This type of organization is one that I would like to work for. *[Talking about the company*]

I am actively seeking employment [*Stating your position*] and my key areas of expertise are:

-
-
-

[*list areas*]

I am a dedicated manager and leader and could make a valuable contribution to your company. I have enclosed my CV and I would appreciate it if you would consider me for employment. [*Stating what your are looking for*].

I will give you a ring in a couple of days so that we can discuss this further. *[The proper ending*]

Very truly yours

[*Your Name*]

FRIENDSHIP COVERING LETTER

Friends are not just your closest and dearest pals, but anyone who knows your name - in fact, anyone who could help you in your job search. Don't rule out anyone prematurely, because they may be able to help you. At this stage it doesn't matter where your friends live, because your friend's friend may live near you!

A great many jobs are filled with people known to the company. Companies can't return employees who don't do a good job; they either have to terminate the contract of employment or start looking for someone else, both of which are expensive. This is why companies are so cautious about employing people and why they so often hire people known to them. Use your friends to help you. You would help your friends if the need arose, wouldn't you?

However, a friendship covering letter is perhaps the hardest of all to write. Friendships are won and lost on poor letter writing, so listed below are five easy steps to make the process a lot easier.

1. **Rebuild old times.**

   Make your reader feel good, and glad that you have got back in contact. State the obvious - if it has been a long time, say so, because he/she is probably already thinking it, and perhaps even thinking that you have a cheek only to get back in contact now that you want something. So, state the obvious:

   'You are probably thinking that it is ages since you have heard from me. You are right, it is a long time - in fact, too long. You are probably thinking I am after something. Well, again, you would be right.'

2. **Explain the situation.**

   Let your friend know what is going on and why you are writing. You simply can't get away with writing 'I need to get out of my present company as things here are unbearable', or 'I don't get on with my boss'. These types of things leave too many questions unanswered. In fact, your reader will automatically think the worst or make things up (for example, that you are in financial debt or that you may have had a mental breakdown). You must come clean and explain the facts. If you are in a dire situation, you can tell people about it in a positive way:

'The company was purchased by (name company) and as there were too many staff I was unfortunately made redundant.' 'I lost my job at the end of (give month).' 'I have decided I need more responsibility so I am seeking to move out of (name company/job) and go into (name field) direct.'

3. **Tell them what you want.**

   This is your chance to paint a clear but brief picture of your desired job. The more detail you give the better. Mention your possible job target; the size and industry of the company; responsibilities and job duties; geographic preferences - in short, anything and everything that is important to you (refer to Chapter 3). Your friends will only be able to help if they know what you are after:

   'My expertise is suitable for (state industry), although I also have considerable background in (state industry). Most of my experience with (name company) was related to (state field) but included materials such as (give examples)'

4. **Ask for advice and ideas**

   Your friends may be able to help:

   'Would you mind reviewing my CV and letters and giving me your honest opinion?'

   However, if they only rub salt in the wounds, ignore their so-called 'advice'.

5. **End on a friendly, enthusiastic note.**

   End the letter on a warm note, otherwise they will see through your approach. Using your friend's name is a good touch:

   'Martin, any assistance you can give me would be gratefully appreciated and I look forward to hearing from you.'

   'I would appreciate it if you could review my enclosed CV. If you know of anyone who might be looking for a salesman or if you have any ideas on where I should direct my job hunt, please could you let me know. With your advice, I might just be in the right place at the right time!'

To sum up, you will increase your chances of success dramatically if you write a really good covering letter, so it is worth spending time getting it just right.

Sample letter

[*Date*]

Mr G Smith

[*The Address*]

Dear George

You may be quite surprised to receive a letter from me because it is ages since we have spoken and years since we last met up. I hope you and the family are all well. [*Establishing rapport*]

A lot has happened since we last spoke and I wanted to make you aware of my decision to leave my current position as Director of Development at [*name company*]. As you know, over the past few years [*name company*], and the defence industry in general, has suffered severe government cutbacks, resulting in redundancies, budgetary controls and a general winding up of the business. These factors have contributed to my decision to look for an opportunity in the civil aircraft business, where the economic climate and corporate outlook are brighter. [*Explaining the situation*]

I believe that my ten years' experience as strategic and development manager have prepared me to plan, manage and run a profitable business, even in difficult times!

I am interested in talking to executives of civil aircraft companies. If you are aware of such opportunities, I would appreciate it if you could let me know. I am not restricted geographically, but if possible I would prefer to be within commuting distance.

I am aware that you must be very busy and I appreciate your consideration. I will give you a ring next week so that we can talk further.

Thanks!

[*Your Name*]

ELEVEN

Conclusion

Congratulations - you have completed this book. Now you have a simple decision to make. You can incorporate the suggestions and ideas presented here into your CV, or you can continue to use that old CV of yours. The choice is simple, but some job hunters just can't be bothered or are too afraid to make the change, even though they are aware that their current CV is not good enough. I hope you are different. Get to work on that CV and all your effort will pay off in the end. Having a job that is right for you is so rewarding.

In summary

- If you want to write a winning CV and are prepared to work on it, you have every reason to expect to achieve it.
- The difference between a winning CV and a mediocre one is small, but you can make that difference now that you know how
- If CV writing doesn't come naturally to you, then take extra time or let us help you by visiting www.perfectcv.com.
- Refer to the sample CVs in Chapter 9 for guidance and ideas. Don't copy, but modify and change them as required.
- Before you commit yourself to another profession, check that it has the potential to challenge and reward you for the rest of your working life.

- Business exists to meet needs, so find a business to meet yours.
- Shed your limitations and enjoy writing about yourself!

The CV review

You have probably found it quite a challenge to complete the exercises in order to write your perfect CV. Now it is time to review and check the quality of this new-look CV, to make any changes and also to give your self-confidence a boost.

1. Is the CV targeted towards the job in question? Is the information geared towards the job on offer?
2. Is there a small personal details section at the top of the CV stating only your preferred name, full postal address, telephone number with STD code, email address, nationality, and marital status?
3. Is there a capability section with three to five capability headings? Are the key requirements of the job addressed in this section
4. Is there a personal capability heading, demonstrating your saleable personality?
5. Are your educational qualifications listed in date order, with the most recent first? Have you included and highlighted the level of the qualification first, and then gone on to include the subject and grades obtained, the establishment attended and lastly put down the year the qualification was achieved?
6. Does the work experience section include dates on the far left and then a space, followed by the job title, company name and location on the same line? Is there a brief description of the company with its size, turnover, profit and management style included? Next, have you indicated who you reported to and how many staff you were responsible for? Have you

given a brief description of your duties and responsibilities? In the achievements section, have you praised and given yourself full credit for a job well done?

7. Have you chosen a covering letter style appropriate to your job search? Is the covering letter written to a named person and does it re-emphasize your levels of expertise?

8. Are the covering letter and CV letter perfect?

If you have answered 'yes' to all of the above, you are now ready to start your job search in earnest. Finally don't forget to write a letter of confirmation in response to each invitation to attend an interview.

Good luck!

Did you enjoy 'Write a Perfect CV in a Weekend'?

Receive a free professional critique of your new CV by emailing a short review of this book to wpcv@careerconsultants.co.uk. Put "Free CV check" in the subject box and send it now!

Contact Sarah Berry

Sarah can be contacted directly by emailing her at
sarah@careerconsultants.co.uk
or by calling (from the UK) 07005 980192

www.careerconsultants.co.uk

Read On...

HOW TO LOVE THE JOB YOU DO

Sarah Berry
£9.99

Is your work life in a rut? Do you feel bored and demotivated? Will you make changes tomorrow, but not right now? If so, this is a disaster because over half our waking lives are spent in our jobs. Read this book and discover how to release a creative spirit at work, find a new purpose, and be more than average. Sarah Berry's 30-day programme is inspiring yet simple and will give you the fuel you need to ignite that job spark now and achieve success at work.

WIN THE JOB AT THE INTERVIEW

Sarah Berry
£9.99

How you perform at an interview will win or lose you the job. Coping with nerves and being prepared will help you to give a good interview performance so that you increase your chances of getting the job and negotiate your salary package if need be. This book helps you to plan ahead and guides you through all the potential pitfalls, so that you are ready for the interview and can give the best possible account of yourself.

HOW TO PLAN YOUR CAREER

Sarah Berry
£9.99

A career is more than just a series of jobs. It requires long-term planning and a sense of direction so that you can decide where you want to go and what you want to achieve. In this book Sarah Berry guides you through the process of structuring your career, from visualizing your goals to identifying the best opportunities for advancement.

HOW TO BE HEADHUNTED

Sarah Berry
£9.99

Not everyone will be headhunted but most people would probably like to be. This practical book shows you how to get to the top. Sarah Berry explains exactly what headhunting is and the procedures involved. She covers everything from becoming a specialist in your chosen field and getting onto a headhunter's files, to the importance of attitude and improving your job performance. This book is ideal for anyone who wishes to progress quickly in their career.

Index